Can you match up these after-school activities?

1. *Hanging around*   a. *Cruising the mall*
2. *Fooling around*   b. *Enjoying a TV show*
                                      while Mom slaves away.
3. *Goofing off*   c. *Acting silly (doing*
                                      dumb stuff)

Of course you can.

But do you know how to keep your faith while indulging in these activities?

In *Cruisin' and Choosin'* you will learn how you can get closer to God while having fun.

●● **By J. Brent Bill** ●●

Rock and Roll
Stay Tuned
Lunch Is My Favorite Subject
Cruisin' and Choosin'

CRUISIN' & CHOOSIN'

J. Brent Bill

Fleming H. Revell Company • Publishers
Old Tappan, New Jersey

Library of Congress Cataloging-in-Publication Data

Bill, J. Brent.
  Cruisin' and choosin' / J. Brent Bill.
    p. cm.
    ISBN 0-8007-5296-8
    1. Teenagers—United States—Social life and customs.
  2. Teenagers—United States—Conduct of life.   3. Dating (Social
customs) I. Title.
HQ796.B448   1989
305.2'35—dc19   88-39416
                                                                          CIP

Copyright © 1989 by J. Brent Bill
Published by the Fleming H. Revell Company
Old Tappan, New Jersey 07675
Printed in the United States of America

Contents

5

Part III: Johnny Bee's Sophisticated System for Dating Members of the Opposite Sex

For Nancy

•• 1 ••
Whachawannado?

"What do you want to do?"
"I don't know. What do you want to do?"
"Doesn't matter to me."
"I don't care either."
"Well, how about we check out what Laurel wants to do?"
"No, I don't want to do that."
"What do you want to do?"
"I don't know. What do you want to do?"

Sound familiar? I'll bet it does. Never in the history of humankind have so many had so much and had so little to do with it. "What is he talking about?" Time, my friend, time. The *average teenager* (though we all know that there's no such critter outside of Disneyland, for the sake of argument, let's pretend there is and that he or she is just like you and your friends) has more time than any teenager ever before and doesn't know what to do with it all.

Oh, I know you feel trapped and pressed for time. There aren't enough hours in a day to do all the things you want. Your life seems to be running from one place to the next doing one thing after another. And I have the nerve to say you have more time than ever before?

Well, it is true. Although you may not know it, as little as one hundred years ago there *were* no teenagers. That's right, people went from 12 to 20 in one step. Okay, so they didn't. But the idea of reserving the years of 13 to 19 for school, play practice, extracurricular activities, and hanging out at the mall is relatively new. One hundred years ago if you were 13 and unemployed, you were a drain on the family. Schooling and stuff like that were for the privileged class. Folks like us who were teenagers were stuck in factories churning out shoes or cutting hay on the farm full-time.

Then society changed and kids started staying in school and having a little more time to grow up. And you are the recipient of all the leisure time created by the sweat of generations of teenagers before you.

Not only do you have more time, you also have more money. The average American teenager has $17,000 disposal income to spend on himself annually. All right, so I made that up. The truth is, you have more cold cash than any generation of kids ever. That's why the record executives at CBS, A&M, RCA, and all the other companies love you and put out albums by the zillion for you. It also explains all the "dead teenager" movies (you know, "hack and slashers" like *Friday the 13th* or *Hallowe'en*). Your parents sure aren't going to them. And neither am I. (Just *having* a teenager gives me all the nightmares I need. Why pay money to get scared?)

Yet, with all this time and money, nobody knows what to do. A common "Benism" (a *Benism* being anything constantly repeated by my resident teenager, Ben) is "I'm bored." And, sad to say, he often is. You may be too.

Another favorite Benism is "School's out!" This is a phrase heard all over the land somewhere between 2:35 and 4:00 P.M. depending on when your school lets out or if you got detention (which none of you would, of course). I think it was George Washington who first uttered this, on his way to Ace Hardware to pick up a hatchet for his after-school job pruning cherry trees. No lie. It has echoed down the hallowed halls of American institutions of education ever since. As far as any teenager is concerned, the last bell really is the best bell. (This view is also widely held by teachers, principals, cafeteria workers, and janitors. School bus drivers are not quite as thrilled.)

The euphoria of being let out of "prison" lasts for about the first fifteen to twenty minutes after we get home from school. Then paralysis begins to set in. We've got homework to do, but don't really want to do it. Our room could use straightening and our bed making, but we did that six months ago and don't want to rush into something so major. After all, we'd just have to do it again in another six months. The grass could be mowed. Nah, the shock would kill Dad. Even TV is boring. You can only watch "The Brady Bunch" so much before it kills off what few brain cells you have trained to think. What to do, what to do. "I'm bored."

Yes, being out of school sounds great when we've still got two periods to go (and one of them is Trigonometry and the other is Classical Latin Poets). But after the first half hour we're bored. We even wish we were back at school, though we'd never admit this to anyone. At least our friends are there. That's it. We've got friends. And friends have ideas. Some good, some not so good. Some our parents will even let us do.

At least they come up with *something* to do. Cruise the mall. Go to a game. Cruise a game.

Everyone wants to do something exciting after school. We all know the only reason the curricular activities exist are so we can go to the *extra*curricular ones. Sure the principal, vice-principal, attendance officers (did you know that in the old days they were called truant officers and could and would come to your home and arrest you!), and teachers think that school exists for learning and classes. But *we* all know that is just not so. Any fool can learn in school. The hard part is doing well in the after-school activities.

We all want something to do when school's out. We don't want to just sit around and we certainly don't want to do anything that is too constructive. After all, we don't want to give teenagers a good name like those guys in the Hall Monitors Club or the girls in Future Homemakers.

What we don't often realize, though, is that what we do after school is as important to our life of faith as what we do in Sunday school. We spend a lot more time doing "fun stuff" than going to youth group, Sunday school, or church camp. We're pretty good at dividing our lives into the "religious" and the "fun." After all, at times, at least from what we've heard at church and from religious types, the Christian motto seems to be "If it's fun, forget it."

You know the folks I mean, the ones who look like their faces would shatter if they smiled. And all the while they are singing songs like "I've got the joy, joy, joy, joy, down in my heart." It sure must be buried deep, because their hearts never give their faces the message.

I believe that Jesus came so you could live life to its fullest. And that includes having fun. In the Bible, He tells us Himself that He came to bring us an abundant life. That includes the after-school, bored, or fun parts. We need to realize that what we do after the last bell's rung says a lot about what we really believe and can teach us more about being close to God. Yes, life is full of lessons that can help us grow, if we just look for them and learn from them. You don't believe me? Well, sit back, Bucko, look at the cartoons, and see if you don't learn something. In spite of yourself.

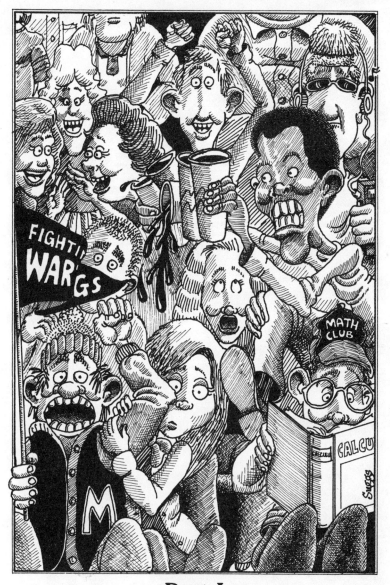

Part I

The Big Game

•• 2 ••

The Pep Rally

"I hear your new boyfriend made the football team."
"Yeah, Jim's so excited."
"What position does he play?"
"I think he said he was one of the drawbacks."

"The ball is on the twenty-yard line. Daugherty takes the snap
for the Warthogs. Napariu of Franklin blitzes the middle,
coming over the center Cortez. Daugherty spots Taylor wide
open at the ten. The pass is wobbly but there. Between Taylor
and the goal line is the meanest defensive back ever to play for
Franklin—Campbell. Taylor fakes for the middle and then heads
for the sidelines. Touchdown, Warthogs."

Sometimes it seems as if the entire school week focuses around
Friday night's game. Who's our opponent? Are they any good? I
sure hope not. If they are, we can pray that their team bus breaks
down on its way over here.

It is easy to "get up" for Friday's big game if we happen to be
playing our cross-county or city rivals. We want to beat them—
and not just by one or two points. We want to pound them by
seven or eight touchdowns and twenty or so field goals. We don't
want just victory, we want *humiliation*. I must say here that this
is not a good Christian attitude. More about that later.

I remember the golden days of autumn, back in the sixties,

when the sky was blue slowly turning to inky black. As the season progressed and a chill hung in the air, the crowds at Magly Field were looking forward to that last climactic game of the year. Our whole school (and anyone who had ever gone there since the thing opened in 1929) got excited when it was time for the final game. For it was then that we played East High. And, since we were West and "West Is Best," there was no lack of emotion generated as the big night approached. When it was time for the East High Buttheads (or whatever they were—none of us bothered to learn their real name; we didn't want to give them that much respect) came across town to our beloved stadium, we were ready. We were *more* than ready. We were ready to whip them and whip them good. We wanted total humiliation. Wailing and gnashing of teeth sort of thing. Sometimes we got it, because it was our football team that didn't live up to our expectations. The wailing and gnashing were our own.

Regardless, we were excited.

It was another matter altogether though when we played some team that couldn't even beat the Westgate Hawks, a Little League Football team made up of physically overgrown, mentally dormant fifth and sixth graders. It is awfully hard to get excited about playing some team that has a hard time making it onto the bus (if they even own one) to come to the game, let alone being a serious contender.

When I was at West, our low-enthusiasm game was our annual rout of the Bishop Ready Crusaders. Believe me, those guys should have worn suits of armor to the game. They needed them. In all fairness, I must report that they have improved and shortly after I graduated they made their trip into West and massacred the Cowboys. I guess if God were going to be on someone's side (like we all think He is on ours), He'd probably go for somebody like the Bishop Ready Crusaders before He would the West High Cowboys.

Regardless of who we're playing, however, there is one pre-game ceremony that is universal and constant. That's the Pep Rally. If we are the favored team, the pep rally's held to keep the excitement growing and growing. If we are the expected victims, it's supposed to inspire us to at least show up for the funeral.

Pep rallies take various forms. Some are held in the gym. They are okay, but not nearly as exciting as the good old-fashioned bonfire-type pep rallies.

A bonfire rally is usually held the night before the big game. As a teenager you like this because it gets you out of homework, housework, and you can stay out late without being pestered. These all rank high on the List of Teenagers' Desired Activities.

To begin, some enterprising young folks volunteer to put together a little bit of wood for the bonfire. The principal always thinks this means they will get some kindling and a few logs from one of the kids' parents' fireplaces.

Wrong.

The difference between what an adult and a teenager define as a little bit is a lot. What it means to the wood-gathering crew is that they will scavenge every board in town that is not nailed down (and a few that are) and set up a bonfire that reaches at least four stories higher than the school building. This they then liberally douse with gasoline or diesel fuel (depending on whether they are members of Future Oil Refiners of America or Future Farmers), "just to get it going." When this thing is lit, fire departments from neighboring states are alerted and little old ladies head for the civil defense shelter, sure that the "bomb" has been dropped.

When the fire has finally gone down enough so that people can stand within a mile or so of it, everyone from school (along with a few juvenile delinquents looking for fun and a couple of old folks in their late twenties or early thirties trying to recapture their lost, misspent youth) begins a grand march to the rally site.

Usually the other team's coach is burned in effigy over the fire, as well. I do remember a group of guys so unsmart (it wouldn't be nice to call them dumb) that they drove around with the dummy of the other team's coach looking for "Effigy" since they heard that it was to be burned there.

"Effigy. Where the heck's that, Stan?"

"I'm not sure, Jon, I think it's up Route 62 somewheres around Leesburg."

They drove around all night, the whole next day, and well into the following week hunting for Effigy. Which, if you'll look on your map, is just down the road from Elkin, south of Mount Airy in North Carolina. Last I heard, those fellas were somewhere in Alabama, having decided to search the country alphabetically since roadside signs had been no help.

After Brigade 16 of the volunteer fire department has the bonfire under control and the ancient, secret, silly high school voodoo rites performed on the other team's coach are over, the real festivities begin. First comes the principal, who gives a greeting that usually sounds something like

"Ahem (blows in the microphone, grossing out the nerd from the A/V lab who's running the system). Is this thing on? (Blows in mike again—feedback from the guy running the P.A., who turns treble and volume all the way up.) Oh, okay. Well, students of Mullenville High—yes, you proud Fightin' Warthogs—welcome to tonight's pep rally. As you know, tomorrow evening our brave lads on the football squad will face off in intraschool gamesmanship against the good people of our beloved sister school, Saint Mattress of the Springs. We wish our boys well and remind you as students that you are representing our fine school and are expected to behave properly. I know you will. Don't do anything I wouldn't do. Ha. Ha."

Everyone promises, with fingers crossed behind their backs, to behave. Of course, they'd promise anything to get the principal to sit down and be quiet.

18

Next come the cheerleaders. The head cheerleader, Buffy Sue Saint Marie, tries to whip everyone into an enthusiastic mood. Sometimes, depending on who the next evening's opponent is, she needs real whips.

"Well, guys . . . and gals, tomorrow's the biggest game in our lives. I'm proud to be a Warthog and I know you are too. So join me and the rest of the cheerleaders and let's all do some really nifty cheers that we made up just for this game."

The cheerleading starts. Fortunately, it is soon over, since the only ones getting whipped into much of anything are Buffy, the cheerleaders, their parents, and assorted school officials. Of course, it is hard to get excited over cheers like

"Come on Warthogs, you can do it,
Belly to the trough and run right through it."

or

"Warthogs, Warthogs,
Come on and snort! Hogs."

Thankfully, Buffy then introduces the team captain, Bill Wright. Bill always has inspiring things to say.

"Well, uh, thanks, uh, Buggy, I mean, uh, Buffy. Well, all I, uh, gotta say, is, uh, tomorrow night, uh, we're going to, uh, kick their—"

"Thanks a lot, Bill," says the principal, wrestling the microphone away from Bill. "Now let's hear from Coach LaPorte."

"Thanks a lot, Dr. Hannon. I just want to say that while tomorrow is a big game, it is just a game. We've got to go out and play them one at a time. Our boys have got to come to play. I just am thankful that I have the opportunity to coach this fine group of young men and will try not to let the team down. It doesn't matter if we win or lose, what matters is how we play the game. Winning isn't everything.

"And come tomorrow night we're going to kick their—"

"Thank you, Coach LaPorte."

At this time, each class gives some sort of class cheer and then the festivities (and the glow from the nearby brushfires) begin to die down. Everyone is excited and ready to grind Saint Mattress of the Springs into the ground. Enthusiasm is at a fever pitch.

What does all of this have to do with our relationship with God? A lot. There are lots of times you don't feel very enthusiastic about your school. You make fun of its name (for us, West High became Waste High). You complain about the food. You hate going to class. Lots of times you'd rather be anywhere but there. Then comes the pep rally on the advent of the big game. Usually that is all it takes to get you up and running and remind you of how you feel. Pep rallies don't really create the feelings, they only recall feelings of loyalty that are lurking deep down inside already. Even on the days you loathe your school, all it takes is for someone from another school to make fun of yours and you're ticked. "Don't talk about my school that way." You're ready to punch him out—or worse, you want to say silly things about his school. And just minutes before, if your best friend asked how you felt about good old Mullenville, you'd just grunt, groan, and slouch lower in your seat.

Sometimes—actually, a *lot* of times—that's how our relationship with God is. We don't feel terribly excited about it. If we're honest, we are less than excited about it. Sometimes we may even wonder if we have a real relationship, since we don't seem to feel anything.

Not to worry. Just as the fact that we aren't always brimming with school spirit doesn't mean we don't care about our school, we don't always have to have feelings to know we're in a relationship—even with God.

Feelings are nice. They let us know that we are alive. But there are times when we don't feel anything about anything, whether it is our school, our best friend, our family, our boyfriend or girlfriend, or God. We can't always live life at a fever pitch. We would burn out. But we know, whether we feel anything or not, that we really do love our school, our best friend, our family, our boyfriend or girlfriend, or God. We *know* that in our hearts, minds, and souls—even when we don't quite feel it.

So next time you're heading home from a pep rally, all fired up and ready to trash the Saint Mattress of the Springs football team, you might want to take time out for a little pep rally for God, knowing that it will remind you of how you feel deep down inside. Remember that though feelings are nice, they aren't the gauge of a true relationship. God is with you even when you don't feel it. He promised.

•• 3 ••

Pre-Game Rituals

"Let's see. When we won the game last week, did I put on my shirt first or my pants first? Mom, are these the same socks I wore last time we won? Good. You didn't wash them, did you? Whew! I don't want all that good luck going out of them. Now where's my lucky towel? I did eat the three bowls of spaghetti and a loaf of garlic bread like I always do, didn't I? Yep. There. Now I think I'm set to go. Wish me luck, Mom."

Rumination of the starting quarterback at home? Nope. Maybe the middle linebacker? Wrong again. These deep thoughts are from the mind of Coach LaPorte.

Ask some jocks (or jockettes) what they do before a game and you will probably uncover a combination of rituals and superstitions that could be included in *Ripley's Believe It or Don't* (the jock version of *Believe It or Not*). They have rituals on everything from what to wear to what to eat to the order things are done in. Though they profess belief in their skill, training, and coach, they don't want to lose on the technicality of not having performed a ritual to the ghosts of Vince Lombardi or Woody Hayes. Once these rituals have been performed, the jocks can enter their fields of play secure in the knowledge that skill and superstition will work hand in hand to bring about a complete and total victory—provided, of course, that everyone else on the team did *their* rituals.

Such thinking is not, and cannot be, entrusted to our valued athletes alone. If you want to be *sure* your team is going to win the big game (or any game, for that matter), a certain number of pre-game rituals must be observed. Otherwise the gods of football will not be happy, and gloom, doom, and general incompetence will be called down upon your hapless warriors of the gridiron.

First, your clothing must be carefully selected. You want to make sure that you are wearing your school's colors. Second, if you are going to the game with others, make sure they are properly attired. This is really crucial. Many teams ranked to win the state championship have been knocked off by a school with a total student body of forty simply because of serious mistakes in apparel. It is imperative to wear your school colors. Make sure the people you are going with are wearing your school colors. Don't even think of the other team's colors. (Thinking in general, and about the other team in particular, is dangerous.) Wearing their colors ensures that your team will lose. I know. It was my fault that the West High Cowboys lost a crucial game by a mere two points during their 1968 season.

No, I didn't trip and fall in the end zone after getting the snap, thereby incurring a safety against us. No, the crowd did not stand up and boo me. I wasn't on the team and most of the disappointed fans didn't even know I was responsible for our team's loss. But *I* knew. You see, I went to the game and I had a date.

Just my having a date did not lose the ball game. It helped, because, after all, if I hadn't had a date we would have won for sure. To understand all of this, you need a little history first.

There were four of us guys who ran around together in high school (a tradition started in seventh grade). There was David Skipper, Greg Bond, Bob Armour, and me.

David was known as "Skipper" because it was his last name (we weren't very original) and because he always drove us wherever we were going, like a skipper. We were his mighty sailing crew. He was brave and sure. We set out one night for a three-hour tour. A three-hour tour. Whoops, wrong story. Actually Skipper turned out braver than any of us thought because after high school and college he became a city policeman. Guns and bullets and all that stuff that can hurt you.

Greg was called "Garglywire" after our frequent mispronunciation of his French class nom-de-plume of *Gregoire*. (We mutilated other French words as well: "oy, oy" for *oui, oui* and "man-sewer" and "madam-wowsal" for *monsieuer* and *madamoiselle*.) He ended up almost dead by being on the wrong end of a gun and bullet and all that stuff that can hurt you, but that happened a few years later and is definitely another story.

Then there was Bob, whom we called either "Robair" after his French name as mispronounced by us, "Fudhead" after a little kid at the library tried to call him Fuzz-head because of his curly hair, or "Bobo" because he dressed kinda like a clown. You see, his pants were always a little loose around his armpits and all of his shirt buttons always buttoned up—to the neck and beyond. Since I have been talking about the importance of dressing you might think it was Bobo who cost us the game. But it wasn't. It was the girl I was dating.

Oh, I haven't said anything about myself. Well, I was as cool and debonair as I am now and dressed the same way I do now. I wore penny loafers, khaki pants, and button-down shirts. My pants stayed on my hips and I always left at least the top button of my shirt unbuttoned. I had many nicknames, but since I am writing this book and "Skipper," "Garglywire," and "Fudhead" are not, I see no reason to humiliate me along with them.

Back to our story.

We were running a little late as we headed out the 3-C Highway to pick up the girl I was dating. Bob had had a little trouble getting oxygen to his brain because his top button was too tight and stretch polyester hadn't been invented yet (it might have saved his life). He had still been trying to tie his wing-tip white tennis shoes (don't ask me where he got them) when we went to pick him up. When he was finally ready he was a sight of sartorial splendor in his wool-blend striped slacks with a tan belt running across the middle of his chest, white cotton dress shirt buttoned to the top, sneakers (after all, this was a casual outing), and black dress socks (after all, he was a member of the Young Republicans Club). At any rate, we were late. My date was ready and impatient. We picked her up and were halfway to South High (You may notice that our school names were not very original: West, East, and South have been mentioned so far. Let me assure you, there was a North. If you wanted a snazzier name you had to go to a Catholic school.) before I noticed how she was dressed. She looked lovely in her pretty white blouse and nice blue skirt with matching shoes and purse. I thought she looked gorgeous. I also thought she'd joined the South High Drill Team. A spy. Dressed for the other team!

The rest of the guys, who were dateless for reasons that may already be obvious, wanted to throw her out of the car right there. I, out of misplaced loyalty to love rather than school, argued that it wouldn't be the Christian thing to do. It was a desperate gamble, but since we were all devout youth group members this appealed to their higher natures. Besides, that way if we lost, it would be my fault. They let her stay in the car. We went on to the game and we lost.

Afterwards, when we went over to where all the South High fans (and my date) were sitting so she could ride home with us, the other guys wasted no time telling her it was her fault we lost. Of course, they did it in a very Christian manner.

The moral of this story then is to dress for success—and make sure everyone around you, male, female or whatever, does, too. If you don't, you may be the one who gets called into Coach LaPorte's office to explain why the team played so well and still lost. Remember, coaches may be adults on the outside, and even teach occasionally, but the fact remains, they believe in all this stuff more than they do Newton's twenty-fifth law of thermodynamics (if there is such a thing).

Of course, rationally, we all (even Coach LaPorte) know that little rituals have nothing to do with winning or losing. What matters is training, being prepared, anticipating what the other team will do before they do it, disguising what you are going to do so they can't guess, and playing your best. But in the back of our minds there are still those superstitions. (Like WTBS in Atlanta? No, that's super*station*, not superstition.)

In our Christian life we may even have little rituals we think help us through life. Like certain prayers:

"God is great, God is good,
And we thank Him for this food."

or

"Dear God, get me out of this
And I'll never do anything bad again."

Or we say,

"I read my devotions precisely at 6:40 A.M. every day."

or

"I carry a Bible with me all the time and never, ever set any other book on top of it."

These, and anything else we do, are kinda God gimmicks. That's not to say there is anything wrong with praying, having a set time for devotion, or carrying a Bible. There isn't. In fact, there is a lot right about all these things. We should pray, have daily devotions, and read our Bibles. What matters is why we do these things.

Just like the things we do before a game really don't influence whether our team wins or not, so too do our little "Christian-isms" have no real effect on whether we win or lose at life. What does matter is whether we are walking closely enough to Him to let Him teach us His ways. We need to spend time walking, talking, and listening to God. Praying, having devotions, and reading the Bible are all ways to be with God if we really want to. If we are just going through the motions as sort of a sacred superstition, they just won't work.

God wants to walk and talk with you. You can hear Him in the deepest part of your life, the part that is the real you. If you want to succeed at life—and I don't mean become rich, or beautiful, or any of those other things the world calls success, what I mean is to have a life you enjoy living—then learn to walk with God. Because if you do, then you needn't worry about superstitions, secular or sacred. I'll bet my lucky rabbit's foot on it.

•• 4 ••

First Quarter

"Oh, say can you see. . . ."

Those are the official opening words to any football game. This is important to mention, because there are some folks who have the mistaken impression that they are the lyrics to the national anthem. They are not. I'm not sure what those words are, but everyone knows that the words preceding any big game are known as the words to "The Sports Song." To prove the point, let's take a look at them now.

Initially, the song begins with a reference to our Hispanic population's influence in sport, asking the musical question, "José, can you see?"—it may be that the sunset or moonrise is in his eyes. "By the dawn's early light" is when the team may finally get to go home after reviewing the game films. "What so proudly we hailed at the twilight's last gleaming" brings tears to any mother's eyes; it's the time just before the game when she last saw her son's uniform clean. "The rocket's red glare" is an obvious reference to the fireworks after each time the home team scores, and "The bombs bursting in air" recalls those mighty throws of our quarterback. Finally, the song winds up with a tribute to one of America's great sports cities, Atlanta—"Home of the Braves."

Another thing that proves this cannot be the national anthem is the way it is treated—always played in twenty-seven different keys by the marching band and lip-synched by the crowd, since no one knows any of the words except for "Oh say can you see" and "home of the Braves." Surely the national anthem would be treated with much more respect.

Immediately after "The Sports Song" the teams take the field. At no other time in a person's life is morality so clear-cut. Out there, staring at one another across opposite forty-yard lines, are good and evil. Saints against sinners. The crusaders against the infidels. Us versus them.

Team names usually gear themselves toward these feelings. This was true for us at West. We were the Cowboys. Having grown up on Westerns, we were culturally prepared to see each game as a glorious reenactment of how the good Cowboy was set upon by the bad Indian and how the good Cowboy, with right, if not always might, on his side, triumphed. It didn't matter that such a myth was falsehood; what mattered was the image presented. Every time we played, we saw our noble cowpokes surrounded by the evil Indians and each victory was a triumph for truth, justice, and the American (although, not Native American) way. Score one for the settlers.

We weren't the only team with a glorious name. There were Vikings, Pioneers, Lions, Tigers, and Bears. Sometimes we were in spiritual combat against Red Devils. Danger lurked behind every helmet. It was easy to get fired up thinking of our valiant Cowboys riding into the sunset, six-shooters blazing and line-backers blitzing.

Other team names make it harder. Take Plainfield, Indiana, for an example. Their team is "the Quakers." "Go fight, Quakers!" doesn't make quite as rousing a cheer. I'm a Quaker, a real one that is, and Ben has played on the junior-high Quaker team, but every time I yell, "Go fight, Quakers," all I can think of is the guy on the oats box and how Quakers are known as pacifists. It seems slightly ridiculous to urge a kindly looking old guy to "Go . . . Fight . . . Kill!" Teams like that are at a disadvantage. It's hard to get intimidated by a bunch of peace-makers.

But no matter what our team's name, it is a battle of the forces of good against the forces of evil. We proudly chant our team's name, whether strong or slightly silly, over and over and over.

"The Sports Song" has been sung, "Go! Fight! Warthogs!" chanted over and over, and then comes the kickoff. As the kicking team races like a runaway train toward the ball and the other team, a huge wailing goes up from the crowd, "Oooooooooooohhh!" ending precisely at the moment when the kicker puts Reebok to Rawlings and the ball soars high into the autumn air, arcing back to earth to land gently and safely in some player's arms. Who is then buried under the other team's entire eleven. The game has begun.

It is easy to maintain interest for the first quarter. After all, the seats for witnessing this contest between good and evil have been selected carefully so you are surrounded by your closest and best friends—or at least people you know. You've had supper, so you aren't going to be hungry for five minutes or so and will probably be able to hold out for at least fifteen. Necessary stops at the little boys' or girls' room are out of the way. Splinters have not yet started their migration from the bleacher to your posterior through your new Levi's, or, if sitting on ribbed, modern metal ones, your rear end doesn't yet look like the mold from which they make corduroy pants.

At first, there's real excitement generated by watching a bunch of guys tearing one another apart just to get at a little leather spheroid, run it around someone's former pasture, and throw it into the ground behind some funny-shaped poles that wouldn't even be good for stringing telephone line. These teenage monsters in their padding and helmets pound, push, pummel, and punish their opponents, mashing them into the mud and grass or giving and getting rug burns from the artificial turf. Back and forth the moral battle wages. The kids stand and cheer when the Warthogs do well, while the principal begins eating his hat when they fall behind. Grown men and women weep when it appears the other team might have recovered our fumble. What do you mean this is just a game? Did the Christians tell that to the lions in the Colosseum? I doubt it. Did they say, "Hey, lion, relax. It's just entertainment"? You can be sure they didn't. It's the same every Friday night at the local high school. Just a game? No, it's war.

Each team and every player knows it, too. The week before the game, every horror story that has ever been told about the other team is retold, amplified, and exaggerated. "Did you know that in the 1947 game Klaus, their middle linebacker, actually bit off our quarterback's nose? Yeah, my grandpa was here then and saw it all."

Yep, it really is good versus evil. I mean, how can they even *let* a team that has players biting off other people's noses in the league with decent people like us? We can't let a menace to all that is good and pure and right win, now can we? We have to win, be victorious. We have to do our bit for ultimate (or at least weekly) moral victory.

You might want to remember that at your next game. When the teams line up and it is your good team versus their evil one, it will be one of the few times that morality will seem so clear-cut. Most of the time in life, choices seem to be shades of gray. Black and white is easier to deal with, but seldom are our decisions in quite that much contrast. To cheat or not to cheat—that may be pretty black or white to us—until we are in the situation that nobody else understands. It may be easy for us to say what we would do, until it is our turn to do it. Sometimes the right moral choices are hard to discern.

I wish that good and evil would line up like the football teams. But sometimes evil jumps offsides. It disguises itself and looks pretty good. Unlike football games, most choices don't have giveaway nicknames or different-colored jerseys to help us tell them apart. What's a person to do?

Learn to think. Inspect your decisions carefully. Try to look at the consequences. And ask yourself how you think God would feel about your decision or what Jesus would do in your shoes. And pray. A lot. The choices you make in life will seldom seem crystal clear. But with God's help you can see the good and the bad for what they are. Then you will be able to choose wisely.

·· 5 ··

Second Quarter

GREAT MOMENTS IN HISTORY

On May 5, 1961, astronaut Alan Shepard became the first American male to leave the earth's atmosphere and soar into space—alone.

On that same day, Elizabeth Pierson, a high school junior, became the first American female to leave her girlfriends' atmosphere and step into a public rest room—alone.

By the time the first quarter ends and just before the second quarter begins, you make an amazing scientific discovery. It has to do with displacement, volume, mass, and other things from the realm of physical science. It also deals with Newton's forty-second law—"For every action there is an equal and opposite reaction." What this means to you at the beginning of the second quarter is that all of the soda you've been drinking since you got to the game is crying for release. You've got to go. I know this is a delicate subject, but it is a natural part of everyday existence for most of us. If it is not for you, you may skip this chapter.

I hate to be a sexist here, but I will be, in order to make a few observations about how males and females deal with "the potty problem." I realize the following statements are generalizations. That doesn't bother me since they are generally true.

Let's begin with the females. Having to visit the "necessary room" is no big deal for a girl. After all, males are always making fun of how often girls have to go to the bathroom. Guys seem to take it as scientific fact that females go to the bathroom more often than males. You could more easily convince them that Einstein's theory of relativity is bunk than that women don't go to the bathroom more often than men. As a matter of fact, many fellas believe Einstein's theory of relativity is that whenever a bathroom is relatively near, a female must stop there.

Such male chauvinistic thinking does have its advantages for women. They can visit the little girls' room whenever they want since it is expected of them. When a girl has to make room for more liquid refreshment, all she has to do is say so. "I'm going to the ladies' room." No one snickers or says anything rude. And instantaneously, thirty-five other females will get up to go, too. Women, young or old, never go to a public rest room by themselves. They always go in herds. Many a male, young boy or old man, has speculated about what fascinating, secret rituals must go on behind the door marked *Women*. Is it the threshold of a secret sorority? Are they plotting world conquest and subjugation of all males? Or do they really just need all that help going to the bathroom?

For a guy it's a little harder. It's hard to feel macho or manly while saying, "I have to go to the bathroom, be back in a minute." And it's even harder in "mixed company," which is a euphemism for more than one member of each of the sexes being together in the same place at the same time, when even euphemisms can't be used. (If you don't know what a *euphemism* is just write a fake note saying you missed class because you had a severe case of euphemism and hand it to your teacher. He or she will be glad to define the word for you.) Guys have to disguise what it is they are up to. And they can't ask their friends to go, because guys don't do that. So Royce will say, "I think I'll just wander around and see who's here," and his wandering will happen to take him by the men's room and he'll decide to see who's there, too.

Lots of visiting goes on during the second quarter—on the way to, from, and in the bathrooms. Especially by the guys, since they have to take such an indirect route to get where it is they really want to go in the first place. You see lots of friends, old and new. You see the guys and gals who graduated last year. and happen to be home from college or have gotten the evening off work. You see people who graduated five years ago and have never grown up enough to quit coming to high school games. Many of them still act like sophomores. You talk to parents of your friends who are on the team and off. The band parents are all there, sitting behind the band or selling booster bars— half-pound chunks of chocolate for the low, low price of $24.95 (financing available, of course). "Sure they are expensive, but they're for a worthy cause."

You also get to talk to members of the opposite sex, away from (if you're lucky) the watchful (read *jealous*) eye of your current love. This can come in handy if your current love is like one of mine was. She may still be, for all I know. I took her to the game and while I was "wandering around to see who's here," she was flirting with every male in the twenty rows around us. And a few in the other team's section, too. By halftime she was sitting with someone else. When the third quarter started, they looked like Siamese twins joined at the lips. At the final gun she was in his car, heading for a night of greasy burgers, fries, and romance. (Actually, I'm not sure about the burgers and fries, but I know the guy she went off with was greasy.)

She did all of this the week before our big homecoming game and dance, for which she was my prospective date. She must not have known that since she did what she did. On the other hand, maybe she did know. At any rate, being the true-blue, loyal, and extremely chivalrous guy I am, I dumped her and asked someone else out. Learn from my mistakes.

Number one: Enjoy meeting potential friends and romantic partners.

Number two: Never go out with girls named Bunny.

The final thing that goes on during the second quarter (other than sporadic watching of the game—"What, you mean a game's been going on? Where? Who's ahead? We are?! When did that happen?") is everyone's getting ready to beat the halftime rush to the refreshment stand. We all know that as soon as the gun sounds ending the half, there is going to be a mad rush to the refreshment stand and, if you go then, you will be stuck there until the middle of the third quarter—of the next home game. So when there are about four minutes left in the half, you see all kinds of people heading for the refreshment stand.

Many of them think they are being clever about it. They say things like, "I guess I'll go stretch my legs," or, "Man, are these seats hard," and then start heading for the aisle. They think they are sneaking off ahead of the rush. But if you took a shot above the bleachers from the Firestone blimp ("Hi, Mom. Bet you hoped I'd forget you called it that!"), you would see there's about as much sneaking here as there was when Moses and the children of Israel hotfooted it out of Egypt. There's not too much that is sneaky about 400 people edging toward the lone outpost that sells consumables. Even if they do say things like, "Isn't that Krista down there? I think I'll go say hello. Be back in two or twenty minutes." Who do they think they are fooling? The other 399 are not flimflammed by this. Everyone knows what's going on.

The sad thing is there is no need to rush. There is no such thing as a halftime crowd at the refreshment stand at a high school game. The halftime rush is just another cruel hoax perpetrated by adults. I'm sorry to disappoint you. First Santa Claus, then the Easter Bunny, and now this. But it is logical. Just think about it. Who runs the refreshment stand at high school games? That's right, the band parents. Those same folks who sell the $24.95 candy bars. Now they are selling sodas for $3.45, stale popcorn for $1.95 a bag, and potato chips so old the cafeteria couldn't even con the freshmen into eating them. And they are the band parents. This is important. Let me repeat it. They are the *band parents*. Now quick. Think. When does the band play? Very good—halftime. What makes you think these folks are going to miss seeing Chris play his tuba or Whitney toss her baton while doing splits. There's no way. The story of the halftime refreshment-stand crowd is a myth devised by the band parents so that no one will come during halftime. They want to see their kids perform.

That doesn't mean you should go to the refreshment stand during halftime though. Not only won't there be a line, there also won't be anyone to wait on you.

Yes, the second quarter is a whole bunch of stuff rolled into fifteen minutes—going potty, visiting with friends, and getting more fuel for the rest of the game. It's a lot like life, which is also a whole lot of different stuff. Some of the stuff is fun—like chatting up some new girl or guy. Some of it's necessary—like going to the bathroom. Just like life. Some of it is fun, some of it is necessary. The only thing guaranteed is that there will be variety.

Sometimes the variety is what makes life hardest. We wish it would all be fun and enjoyable and it's not. Things always happen to take the fun out of it. We have homework and housework to do, rooms to clean, yards to mow, snow to shovel, little brothers and sisters to baby-sit, and on and on and on. And of course, there's school. Up early each morning and endure until late each afternoon. "Gee, I sure wish it were Friday." And that's at 8:10 Monday morning.

The only trouble with, "Gee, I wish it were Friday" at 8:10 Monday is that we are putting our lives on hold until Friday comes. Two things can happen. One is that Friday will come and, for all of our wishing for it, it won't turn out as neat as we hoped it would. It won't be quite the salvation we prayed for.

The second thing is that we will miss the things that are going on while we are on hold. Life keeps happening. By mentally and emotionally checking out, we miss a whole lot of life. Even in the drudgery, there might be some excitement. We get so busy thinking about the future that we miss out on the present. The thing we need to learn to do with life is to ask God to help us enjoy the variety—the fun and the necessary. That won't necessarily make the necessary fun, but it might show that fun isn't always necessary. Life has to be fully lived if we wish to live it fully.

·· 6 ··

Halftime

"The gun sounds and that's the end of the first half. The Fightin' Warthogs lead Gas City 28 to 3. And now, coming onto the field, is the Mullenville High School Band, the Marchin' Warthogs, under the direction of Dr. Robert McWeeney. Drum major for the Marchin' Warthogs is Timothy Higgenbotham, and the head Hogette is Madeline Elkin. Welcome, won't you please, the mighty Marchin' Warthogs."

You thought you'd seen a well-prepared team before. Well, now coming onto the field you'll see a bunch of kids even better drilled than the football team. The team may yell about two-a-days or three-a-days, but the band has all-a-days. The guys on the football team at least have tackling dummies and one another to take out frustrations on. What's someone in the band going to do—fight a flutaphone? You may not believe it but it is harder to get in the band than on the football team. Football players don't like to hear that, and probably don't believe it, but it's true. And it is even harder to stay in the band than on the team.

Think about it. If someone on the team makes a mistake, everybody says it's too bad, thumps them on the helmet or pats their rear end. Even Coach LaPorte, as soon as he's done eating his clipboard, says, "Hey, dat's okay. Ya gave it all ya got out dere."

Even the fans know that errors will be made. In a close game you can hear one knowledgeable dad tell another, "The team that makes the fewest mistakes will win." Sports is filled with all sorts of adages like that. Band competition, however, is not.

Band directors make even the most fearsome coach look like a kindly old grandfather. They are dictatorial in their power and use of it. In football, at least theoretically, a player can scrap the coach's play if it is apparent that it won't work in a particular situation or if a good opportunity comes along. If it works, the coach will love you—and claim it was his all along. If it doesn't, you'll get screamed at. So what. The coach is always screaming anyhow. And the only ones who know about the change are the coach and the guy who brought in the play.

In band, though, if you deviate from the plan, everyone knows. That's because the people in the stands all see you doing something unique. The rest of the band has stopped and you've kept going, mowing down two clarinets, four trumpets, one trombone, finally bringing your tuba to rest against the bass drum—which *can't* move. Not only does everyone in the stands see it, it is also replayed on the local news at eleven o'clock. Everyone in four counties knows you messed up.

This tends to make the band director look bad. It makes him look like he doesn't know what he's doing. This makes him upset. Angry, even. Downright crazy. Homicidal. He takes it out on you.

That's the reason for all those all-day, everyday practices. Drilling, drilling, drilling. You do the same thing over and over and over again. Being in the marching band is about discipline, discipline, discipline. It is repetition, repetition, repetition.

Have I made the point about repeating? I hope so, because I'm getting tired of writing the same words over and over and over. Ooops, there I go again. But there is a reason for the repetition. If you do things over and over you begin to learn simply because you have done them over and over. You learn to turn here, spin there, or whatever by reflex, without even thinking about it. By sheer rote, you have learned complicated maneuvers and choreography and how to keep playing while doing them all. All because you did them over and over and over. . . . You don't have to think. Which is fine with your leader, because the band director's motto is "You are not here to think, but to do."

That's okay in band. In fact, it's necessary. But in life, it's not necessary and it is not good. The last thing you want to do in life is just go through motions without considering what it is you're doing. God gave you a brain, not a band director. I suppose He could have given us band directors and trained us by repetition. Practice, practice, practice. But that's not the case.

God is more like the coach than the band director. You have a chance to quarterback your life. Look over the other team and see what play fits the current situation. What may fit one time, may not work another. In band it is good to be locked into certain choreography and motions. It looks pretty from the Firestone blimp. But in life, simply going through steps and preplanned motions that we do because we don't even think of doing anything else ("I've always done it that way") may take us places we don't want to be. You also might find yourself blindly following the crowd and not liking where they are going. And not knowing how to get where *you* want to go.

So while the band plays on, appreciate the training, practicing, repetition, and discipline it takes to do what they are doing. But at the same time, thank God for having a team and not a band.

"And a-one and a-two. . . ."

•• 7 ••

Third Quarter

"And as both teams charge back onto the field, a huge snore goes up from the crowd."

The third quarter is about to begin. The band has finally left the field, but only because the principal threatened to call the governor and have the National Guard come and drag them off. The fans have settled back into their seats. Strategies have been discussed and screamed in the locker room. But all is not well.

The first and second quarters and halftime are over. Danger is around us. During the third quarter, fatigue begins to set in. Silly mistakes start occurring. Things that have been practiced and practiced to perfection start going wrong. No, I'm not talking about the quarterback throwing an interception or the defensive tackle missing the count and jumping offside. Those things may be happening too, but I'm talking about what's happening in the stands. The fans are getting tired. Interest is all but lost. A general malaise sets in (probably part of a warm front coming in from Malaysia). Bad things are happening to good people.

Let's look at an example. You may have been unlucky enough to take a date to the game who doesn't know anything about football. Furthermore, she doesn't want to know anything about it. She just went to the game to be with you. This is bad for you and for her.

It is bad for you because you get tired of explaining everything. Sure it was fun for the first two minutes. You got to be the expert, enlightening her on the arcane mysteries of the game. You were a veritable fount of knowledge. It may all have been wrong, but she didn't know. She was a sponge, soaking up all your fountain was putting out. But this gets old. Very old. After all, you want to watch the game, and how can you watch the game when you are constantly explaining something to your date? Early in the game, every time she asks you a question, you turn to her and explain, as simply and slowly as you can, what just happened. This means you are looking at her. If you are looking at her, you're not looking at the game. So you miss three or thirty plays, depending on how simply and slowly you have to explain everything. Pretty soon you quit looking at her while you talk. That way you can explain and watch at the same time. Pretty soon after that you quit talking and mutter something like, "Ask your brother when you get home." You're tempted to buy her a gift subscription to *Football Digest*, just so she'll let you watch the game. That's when it turns bad for her.

Remember, she's only there for one reason. She just wanted to go with you. So after two fifteen-minute quarters, which each lasted about twenty-five minutes, and the halftime show with the band extravaganza, by the time the third quarter starts, your date has been with you for sixty-five minutes. For sixty-three of these minutes you've been focusing on a bunch of people scurrying around on lime-lined grass. And now you are not even looking at her when you speak. You've handed her a copy of *Introduction to Football* and told her to read it. These things are not conducive to a good time being had by all. It could kill a relationship. The only reason she asked questions was to get your attention. "Why do they call it *football* when they carry it in their hands?" and "Why does that guy have his hands under the other guy's rear end?" are only attempts at conversation. Deal with these early or the next one you hear will be, "How much longer are we going to be here?" This last one is repeated over and over and soon you, fatigued, say something like, "Why don't you just watch the game and figure it out yourself?" This is the kind of mistake I was talking about earlier. It could cost you the game (date)—and the next six, if your date tells her friends about you. Fan error.

Coordination begins to slip, too. Everybody is getting thirsty, so you volunteer (sometimes to get away from the "How much longer" questions) to go get everyone something to drink. You do this because you can walk real slowly and keep watching the game. You can even stand in the runway of the stadium and peer out at the action.

Of course, when you volunteer, you're always sitting in the middle of the bleachers. This means stepping over everyone to get to the aisle, which is forty-eight people away. In each direction.

> "Excuse me. Pardon me. Sorry about stepping on your hand. Excuse me. Oops, was that your little boy? Pardon me. Ohh, I didn't realize that was your wig on the ground, ma'am. I thought a squirrel got in."

This is hard enough when you have nothing in your hands. When you come back, laden with thirteen 5-ounce Cokes (actually 4.5 ounces of ice and .5 of Coke), it's even harder.

You begin the trip back carrying these thirteen drinks in four three-cup holders that you had to leave a five-dollar deposit or your driver's license for. They are supposed to make carrying the drinks easier. They even look like they were designed to hold cups. They do. But not as many as you have. ("I'd give you another one, but we just ran out.") And not the size cups they gave you. The material used to make a cup holder is designed to melt if it comes in contact with a carbonated beverage. With pop. With soda. With a soft drink. With what you just bought, okay? When some of it gets spilled, and it always does, a chemical reaction begins and turns the cup holder into something with the sturdiness of overcooked spaghetti.

You start back with a holder in each hand and one clenched in your teeth. And remember, they only hold three cups, so you're probably balancing one on top of your head, too. All goes well for the first two steps. Then a little soda comes out of the plastic tops that don't fit the cups. ("I'd give you the right size, but we just ran out.") This happens to the one in your mouth first. It begins to droop. You tilt your head back. Coke runs out of the top of the cup, down the holder, across your upper lip, and into your left nostril. The fizzies start up your sinuses. There is nothing you can do. You can't sneeze. You can't put a hand up to stop you from sneezing. You decide you'd better hurry on up to the 211th row before something bad happens. You speed up. You can't see where you are going.

"Excuse me pardon me excusemepardonmeexcusemepardonme. . . ."

Glancing down around the container clenched not so firmly in your mouth, you try to read the row numbers.

"208, 208a, 209, 209a, 210, 209a (slipped on a piece of ice, miraculous recovery), 210, 210a, 211."

Aah, home at last. Your arms are giving out from balancing the other two holders and the one in your mouth would be down to

45

your bellybutton if you didn't have your head tilted so far back that if it rains you'll drown. Only forty-eight people to climb over.

"Excuse me, pardon me, sorry about your kid again lady, excuse me."

Finally, the end is near. Two people to go. Then that sneeze you've been stifling will stifle no longer. Aaaah-choooooooooooo. Everything goes. You drop it all. It lands right at your feet and Coke and ice go shooting fifty feet into the air like a soda pop Old Faithful. It all comes down on your date. And the person in front of you. Who is the biggest, meanest, ugliest guy in the stands. It shoots down the back of his neck with the accuracy of William Tell's arrow. Of course, this guy is not happy. This is a person who eats people for snacks before study hall. You want to help clean him up but are afraid to touch him. There is nothing to do but mutter inane words, ask your friends to call the mortuary, and pray that the end will be quick. If you're lucky, you live. He's too mad to kill you. He just glares a lot. You try to melt into the bleacher wood. And then your date says, "I'm thirsty. How much longer?"

Fatigue and mistakes are a part of all of our lives. Sometimes we just don't want to get out of bed, we're so tired. And when we do, we do something stupid. That's okay. It's part of being human. And God understands that. He's used to humans not being perfect. Or even being a lot less than perfect. Even being bad. After all, some of the "heroes" of the Bible would hardly be heroes anywhere else. Even the good guys like David seem to stumble and fall somewhere along the line. God understands. That's one thing that has been constant about God's relationship with us—He loves us and we keep messing up.

It's hard to make mistakes. Actually, it's easy to make mistakes.

We know that's true, otherwise we wouldn't make so many of them. What I meant to say is that it is hard on us when we make mistakes. We like to be perfect—or at least appear so to everyone around us. We feel so stupid when we mess up. Some of us feel stupid a lot. But it really is okay to make mistakes. It is just not okay to keep being down on ourselves for failing. Failure, unfortunately, is a part of all of our lives. God understands that better than we do.

So keep the faith, even though life is sometimes discouraging. God understands our mistakes and loves us just the same. And if God is on our side, we can't help but win.

·· 8 ··

Fourth Quarter

"Okay, guys, this is it. The end is near. This is the grand finale. The whole enchilada. . . ."

"An enchilada? Hey, Coach LaPorte, is the game over? Are we going to eat now? I'm hungry."

"For goodness sakes, Mike, it's just a saying. Go back to sleep. I'll wake you if we need you on a play. The rest of you guys, listen up. We're going to take this quarter one minute at a time. The score's 24–3. We've got them right where we want them. With this kind of a lead, they are bound to be a little cocky. So let's get out there and score points. Pleeaaase!"

The fourth quarter. There is almost as much excitement here as when the game began. It all comes down to this, the last fifteen minutes—which will last at least forty or so.

For an entire autumn evening, two teams have battled up and down, back and forth, over a piece of ground that used to look as manicured as your grandfather's front lawn. Now all that beautifully maintained turf looks like a bad day at the pig auction. Where the pigs won. Uniforms that were once brightly colored are now all the same sheen of grass stain and dirt. Helmets that gleamed in the fading sunset now are battered and marred with the paint of the other team's colors as a result of forty-five minutes of butting heads. The players themselves are wearing new colors—blacks and blues and ugly, bruise yellow.

The coaches, who, at the beginning, looked neat and clean and in control, are now pacing the sidelines like madmen—hats askew, shirttails flapping in the fall breeze, ripping out handfuls of hair. Cheerleaders have frenzied themselves and the fans out. A sort of state of shock has settled over the stadium. Football battle fatigue. Pre-post-game syndrome. A giant letdown. The fans look like they are rehearsing for a part in a Sominex commercial.

Then something happens. One of the teams does something to tip the battle toward or away from them. Their quarterback misreads the coverage. He fakes a handoff to the fullback up the middle. He drops back and fires one across the line. Your middle linebacker steps into the seam. He intercepts and races downfield for the score. Screams of celebration erupt from your side of the stadium. Groans well up from theirs. Your team tries an onside kick—and fails. Their man fields it and, running deftly behind his blockers, streaks down the sidelines. Your one hope is the kicker. Who never tackles anyone, because last time he did he didn't wake up for thirteen weeks. He hesitates. Thinks it over. Thirteen weeks of no school doesn't sound so bad. He lunges for the runner. Grabs his arm. Causes a fumble and recovers it. The crowd goes wild. Your team is only down 24–20. But there are only twelve seconds left.

"The Fightin' Warthogs have the ball on their own 2½-yard line. It looks bad, fans. Chilcoat is lined up slot left. Walters is at fullback. Guzzo takes the snap. Hands to Walters who heads for the line. Wait a minute!! He pulls up, fires down the sideline to Chilcoat. He's got it at the 25! He's got two Wildcats to beat. He cuts to the middle and then back to the sideline. Faked one out of his jock, uh, socks. Now at the Wildcats' 45 he's got only the free safety to beat. It's going to be a footrace. He's at the 35, 30, 25, 20, 15, 10; the free safety lunges at him—and misses. He's at the 5 and now scores! The gun sounds. Holy cow! How about that, sports fans. What a barn burner!"

The fans go wild. Your date hugs and kisses you. You wish your team could score again. Coach LaPorte starts stuffing his shirt into his pants, turns his hat around right, quits chewing on the blackboard, and generally tries to look like a human being again. After all, that's how he designed that play. The team is carrying Chilcoat off the field on their shoulders. The other team is sitting on their helmets, staring at the ground, trying not to cry because football players don't cry, no matter how bad they feel. If even one tear hit the ground, Dick Butkus would come give them something to cry about. They'd have to watch him on another TV show.

Yes, victory is sweet. But we don't always win. Even though Vince Lombardi supposedly once said, "Winning isn't everything, it's the only thing," we usually lose as often as we win. That's hard to take.

But we need to know that God loves losers, too. He must since He made so many of us. Losing is just part of life. It is what you *do* with your losing that really makes you a loser or a winner. How do you handle defeat?

When things don't go your way, do you cry and whine and give up? I do, sometimes. I hate to admit that, but I do. Sometimes we do feel like just sitting down, pounding sand, and crying our eyes out. Sometimes we do more than just feel like doing that, we actually do it. But usually we don't.

Nobody likes to lose. And I wish I could tell you that you never will. But you'd know I was lying. Losing is a part of life. Some of us lose more than football games; we lose friends, lovers, parents. Sometimes we lose because of something we did or didn't do. We lose friends because of something we said or didn't say. Other times, we lose and nothing we could have done would have affected the outcome. Like when our parents get divorced.

There are times we lose and we just don't understand why. "If God really loved me, I wouldn't feel so lousy." Well, the truth is that God does really love you, and you are still going to feel lousy sometimes. But at least you have God to turn to. Some folks don't. Not because He isn't there for them, but just because they don't know that they can turn to Him.

Yes, victory is sweet. But how do you handle life's defeats? If you feel like pounding sand, go ahead. Remember, though, that God is probably sitting next to you pounding sand along with you, *for* you. God is with you, and for you, whether you lose or win. That makes life a no-lose situation.

Part II
Foolin' Around

.. 9 ..

Hangin' Around

"Hang around, hang around,
I hang around."

—the Beached Boys
from the album
Seemingly Endless Summer

Hangin' around is a favorite American pastime. For some of us, it is our only pastime. But that's another chapter. Maybe even another book. One reason hangin' around is so popular is that you can hang around a lot of different places. You can hang around home, your friend's home, the mall, your school, or the swimming pool. But hangin' around is not just limited to "ats", like "*at* McDonald's" or "*at* the football field." You can hang around with "its", too. As in, "I'm going to hang around with Mark" or Lori or Pat. Yes, you can even hang around with people. And generally, people are more fun to hang around with than animals. Although some *are* animals. Still, all in all, I would rather hang around with people than with anteaters. I bet you would, too. Unless, of course, you *are* an anteater. Then you would rather hang around with other anteaters. Or better still, ants.

Since you are a humanoid, we're going to talk about hangin' around from a people standpoint. Your primary qualification for hangin' around is having no plans. If you have plans, you cannot hang around. Read on to see how a good, hangin'-around time is ruined by a guy with plans.

Carl: "Hey! Whatcha gonna do?"
Teddy: "I'm going to the Cinema XXII to see *Jaws 19—The Revenge Gets Revenged.*"
Carl: "Oh."

A perfectly good hangin'-around time has just been wiped from the boards by some fool who had plans. This is how a hangin'-around decision-making conversation should go.

Carl: "Hey! Whatcha gonna do?"
Teddy: "Uh, nuthin'."
Carl: "Wanna just hang around?"
Teddy: "Hey, why not."

It is also important to not get too excited about "just hangin' around." Think about it. If you had something more exciting to do you'd be doing it. But you don't want everybody else to know that you don't have something more exciting to do. If someone asks you, "Wanna hang around?" and you go, "Oh, boy! Do I ever!!!" that's pretty much a dead giveaway that you did not have anything too awfully special already planned. Answer everything in a monotone. Show no emotion. You're a teenager so you're probably already pretty good at this. Just pretend you're talking to your parents. The "How was school, dear?" "All right." form of conversation you have with your mom is a good rule of thumb.

A really good thing about hangin' around is that it's a nonspecific activity. It allows a lot of freedom. If you are hangin' around you can then go to the mall, shoot hoops, go swimming, play cards, or go to the movies. In other words, it can go from nonspecific to real specific, depending on your mood while you're hangin' around.

The possibilities of things to do while hangin' around are limited only by your imagination. And that, since you are a teenager, we all know is limitless. I mean, just look at the excuses you've come up with for your parents on why you've done the things you've done. If *they* don't take imagination, nothing does.

There are different types of hangin' around—from basic hangin' to advanced hangin'. In basic hangin', you do just that. You just hang around. Doing nothing. You wait for something to happen. You wait and wait and wait. You can't *make* it happen. That's against the rules. Sometimes you wait for five minutes, other times, five days. It can get pretty boring. Basic hangin' is okay for freshmen and young sophomores, but if you are a senior and find that most of your hangin' around is still of the basic variety then you had better sign up at your local School of Teenage Living for a class in Remedial Hangin' Around. To be seventeen and still in basic is not good.

The next type of hangin' around is intermediate. Variety comes into play here. You don't just hang around. You don't say, "Let's hang around." The freshmen are doing that. You say, "Let's hang around at your house," or, "Let's hang out at the mall." Intermediate hangin' around usually begins when some-one in the group reaches 16 and gets his or her license to kill, uh, er . . . drive. This gives you and your buddies the freedom to do *site shopping*, an integral part of intermediate hangin' around. You want to shop for the perfect place to hang around. You don't want to hang around at Burger King if everyone else is at the Rax on the other side of town. With wheels you don't have to. But they have to be wheels driven by a teenager. After all, no mother in her right mind is going to take you one place to just hang around. Don't even think of asking her to take you site shopping. Face facts, parents aren't going to help you in your quest for the ultimate hangin'-around spot. They don't like you and your friends just hangin' around the house, and they sure aren't going to help you hang around where they can't keep an eye or two on you. Seriously, now. Can you imagine the following conversation taking place anywhere but on TV?

> "Say, Mom, after supper would you take Tom and Dave and me to the mall?"
> "Why, honey? Is there something you need?"
> "Naw. We just want to hang around."
> "Why sure, Randy dear. Just let me finish clearing the dinner table, taking out the garbage, and loading the dishwasher while you rest up and then I'll run you out."

Talk about a fantasy situation. I don't know how to tell you this but they did have cars and shopping centers (that's where people went to shop in the pre-mall era) and even McDonald's when your mom was a teenager. She used to hang around, too. She remembers those days. And what she used to do. There is no way on God's good earth she is ever going to let you do the same things she did. And don't even try your dad. His memory may not be as good as Mom's but what little is still functioning is just as lethal. He went hangin' around, all right. Probably with your mom. But just because they hung around as kids doesn't mean they'll encourage you or help you in this important teenage pursuit.

So, when Jerry gets his license and can borrow a car (caution: do not say, "Can I borrow the car to go hang around." This does not work), you are free to learn the exciting world of intermediate hangin' around. You can hang around the mall or malls if your town has more than one. You can hang around McDonald's, Hardee's, Wendy's, Burger King, and back again. Multiple hangin' around burger joints is not recommended, however, as managers of these places tend to get uptight and throw you out.

Especially if you are eating a Whopper at Wendy's or a McDLT at Hardee's.

By late in your junior or early in your senior year you are ready for advanced hangin' around. This is the most creative of all the hangin' arounds. To see if you are ready for advanced hangin' around, take the following PHAT (Pre-Hangin' Around Test). Simply score each of the following statements either "B" for basic, "I" for intermediate, or "A" for advanced. You have fifteen minutes for the test. Use a number two pencil and make sure you darken the answer completely. A computer will not be used to grade this test. Answers will be given immediately following the test. When you have completed the test, hand in the answer sheet to yourself. There is to be no talking.

1. Let's hang around. B I A
2. Let's hang around at Debbie's. B I A
3. Let's hang around at Baskin-Robbins and ask the clerk to name all the flavors and then order vanilla. B I A
4. Wanna hang around? B I A
5. Wanna hang around at the Glendale Mall? B I A
6. Wanna hang around at the Greenwood Mall and walk up the down escalator at Sears? B I A
7. Wanna hang around the swimming pool wearing our moms' swimsuits to see if we can get anybody to laugh? B I A

Scoring: Questions 1 and 4 are B, questions 2 and 5 are I, and questions 3 and 7 are A. Question 6 was a trick question, because even first graders from Central Elementary School can come up with that. I know because one lives with me.

The thing to remember while hangin' around, though, is that somebody is watching you. Often you aren't even aware of it. Or you think it is silly that somebody would be watching you. But they are. You watch them. We all like to watch what other people are saying and doing. It's fun. It shows us a little more what they are like. That's scary, isn't it?

So people are watching us—when we're at school, home, work, or hangin' around. They probably know that we go to church and claim to be Christians. So what is our hangin' around showing them about the Christian life? Is what we are doing while hangin' around reflecting something that pleases God or not? Is where we hang around good? Are the people we hang around with the people we ought to hang around with? Do they help us or hurt us?

People watch what we are doing. They want to see if we, who claim to be Christians, are really any different than they are. If we are just the same as they, why should they want to join the Christian life? Our actions—from helping an elderly person wash windows to heckling the other team's fans—say something about how far we let God into our lives. We can lead the people who are watching us into a relationship with God if we are reflecting something they would like to be. So, next time you plan to go hang around, answer this question: "Is your hangin' around good, clean fun or malicious?"

Whether you are a beginning, intermediate, or advanced hangin' arounder, remember what you do reflects who you say you are. Wanna go teepee someone's house with me?

·· **10** ··

Foolin' Around

"I know, first we'll walk backwards through the mall talking like Donald Duck, then we can inhale some helium and talk funny, then we could go to the airport and quote Bible verses to the Hare Krishnas and then—"

"Gee, I don't know if my folks will let me do that kind of stuff, Grandma."

To the inexperienced, it may seem that hangin' around and foolin' around are the same thing. This is especially true to a nonteenager, also known as an adult. However, as all true teenagers know, there are major differences between hangin' around and foolin' around. These differences, so obvious to a teenager, will be explained fully for any adults who may have picked up this book by mistake, thinking it was *Redbook* or *Field & Stream*. (Mistakes this glaring are often made by adults because they have lost the ability to think—usually because their brains have gone dead trying to outthink teenagers at home and the boss at work. If confronted with their mistake, they will deny it, saying "No, I just wanted to see what kind of trash you were reading now." Assure them that this is trash of the highest order and let them read on. They may learn something that will help you.)

Hangin' around can be largely passive or inactive, as we discussed in the previous chapter. Hangin' around usually consists, at its most basic, of doing things like "Let's hang around the house and watch TV." Foolin' around, on the other hand, is active, not passive. Foolin' around means doing something. We will explore this concept more fully as the chapter progresses.

Hangin' around also has no implied emotional content, either serious or humorous. Foolin' around implies having fun. Usually in silly ways. Hence the word *foolin'*. Foolin' around is all about doing dumb stuff. Or being stupid. A friend of mine once described his formative years this way:

"When we were teenagers we used to be stupid a lot. We grew up in Nebraska and there wasn't much else to do but be stupid. So we were stupid a lot. Boy, was that fun."

Believe it or not, this man who spent the largest part of his teenage years being stupid is now senior pastor of one of the leading churches in a large midwestern city. And I am glad to tell you that there are times when he is still stupid. This is something he tries to hide from most of his church members though. After all, no one wants to say, "You just have to meet our pastor. He's so stupid." (Although many parishioners may think that at times.)

Now, being stupid has nothing to do with really being stupid (even though your parents might think it does—"What did you do that for, are you stupid?"). Being stupid is a state of mind. It is important to fooling around. You can't fool around if you are in a smart state of mind. You must feel like being stupid before you can really fool around.

Foolin' around is also extremely creative. It is like advanced advanced hangin' around. You can do some of the same things you would do hangin' around, but to make them foolin' around you have to add a twist. Check out the following examples.

1. To go shoot some hoops is not foolin' around.
2. To let the air out of the basketball, fill it with helium, and then shoot hoops is foolin' around.
3. To go out to the mall is not foolin' around.
4. To go out to the mall, make up words, and act like you're foreign exchange students from Upper Vulgaria and speak nothing but Upper Vulgarian to other shoppers and storekeepers as if trying to find a bathroom, that is foolin' around.

Foolin' around is about having fun. Sometimes it means cutting loose and being somebody you're not. Or somebody your girlfriend or boyfriend or parents wish you weren't. Really, it is being somebody you are but usually aren't encouraged to be.

"Quit being stupid."

"Stop acting that way, you're embarrassing me."

How often have you heard those phrases? Face facts. Sometimes you are embarrassing and stupid. Sometimes that is the real you. We aren't *always* well mannered, or smart, or the way everyone else wants us to be. Sometimes girls (and boys) just want to have fun. And that's okay.

You need to learn to like yourself—all your different selves. No one is just one person all the time. Foolin' around gives us a chance to express a side of ourselves we may not often let come out in public. Of course, if you are always in the foolin' around stage you are shortchanging the other sides of you.

Yes, we are different people at different times. Sometimes we are serious, like in church. Sometimes we're silly, like with our friends at the amusement park. Other times we're scared—just before the big test, for example. And sometimes we are silly when we shouldn't be, like when we get the nervous giggles at a funeral.

We have lots of different ways of acting and feeling. Sometimes they are appropriate to the occasion, other times they're not. But it's nothing to worry about. We have to learn to like ourselves for all the different people we are. That combination is unique. That particular blend is what makes me, me, and you, you.

Maybe you feel like foolin' around now. If you do, remember that God made you in all your smartness and silliness. Rejoice in that. Maybe when God thought you up He was in a foolin'-around mood and that's why you are the way you are. What a stupid thought.

•• 11 ••
Goofin' Off

"Son, your mother and I want you to know how proud of you we are. You did so much after school today. You cleaned the entire house, washed both cars, did all the laundry, trimmed the hedges, ·helped your little brother with his homework, straightened the garage, got Mrs. Herbkersman's cat out of the tree, swept off the—"

"Scott, Scott—wake up, wake up. The way you were screaming you must have been having a terrible nightmare."

Goofin' off, contrary to how it sounds, has nothing to do with being goofy. I mean, you would think any phrase that has *goofin'* in it would have something to do with being silly. This is just not true in this case. Though *goofy* and *goofin'* are derived from the same word, careful etymological study (if you don't know what that means, look it up—this is not a textbook even though I hope you learn something) reveals that the root word from which *goofy* and *goofin'* both sprang is *gauvin*. This is an old French word. Its original meaning is "to avoid work," as in *J'est t'me oui a gauvin*. The word *goofy* is a corruption of some Middle-Ages (as opposed to middle-aged, though he might have been that, too) French peasant's cry to his feudal lord. Almost all teenagers, though striving to appear illiterate, know the origins of most words and hence use *goofin'* in its best sense—to avoid work.

Goofin' off—avoiding work—is a major teenage pastime. It usually ranks somewhere between hangin' around and foolin' around in actual hours per week. It takes a lot of time and skill to goof off. If you're not careful you end up actually doing some work. This is not good. If your friends find out, your reputation will take such a setback, it will take years of doing nothing but hangin' around, foolin' around, and goofin' off to recover. Be alert.

Parents are forever telling kids that "hard work never killed anybody." It is the smart teenager who doesn't take any chances. You'd hate to be the first, wouldn't you? And think of your parents. The guilt would kill them.

> "Oh, Megan, it's all my fault. I kept after Jonathan to clean his room. 'Hard work never killed anybody,' I always told him. And then, to walk in and find him dead, with the vacuum cleaner roaring away and a can of Lemon Pledge shooting off into space. I'll never forget that scene. And it's all my fault. It's all my fault. It's all my fault. . . ."

Maybe you could live with that on your conscience if you were dead, but I couldn't. Don't—I repeat—don't take any chance of killing your folks off by doing something stupid like cleaning the garage or taking out the trash without being hounded into it. Though tempting at the time, it's just not worth it.

Besides, goofin' off, avoiding work, is hard work. It's a lot harder than just giving in and doing the work would be. It requires the use of a person's entire faculties to come up with clever ways to goof off. Avoiding work is work. Adults don't seem to appreciate that. They are always saying things like

> "You spent more time avoiding that job than it would have taken to do it."

or

> "If you had gone ahead and done it it would be over by now."

Adults miss the point. How much imagination does it take to go ahead and do the job? How much creativity would be lost by not thinking up excuses for getting out of work? Sure you spent more time avoiding the job and it would have been over by now if you had done it. Parents are always telling you to use your head or think things through, and here, when you do, they don't appreciate the effort that you put forth. Don't you just wish they'd make up their minds?

The main point is not to avoid work (although that is a noble goal indeed), it is rather that it is a kid's moral responsibility to avoid work as long as teenagerly possible. We all know we have been placed on this earth for a reason. We've heard that in Sunday school since we were little. The older you get, the clearer your reason for existence becomes. As a child, it is to bring happiness, mirth, and joy to your parents and other adults.

"Oh, look at little Amanda. She's so-o-o-o cute when she sits in the toilet like that and flushes it."

When you are a teenager your reason for existence is to turn your parents into idiots. Fortunately, this is not hard.

Parents are on the brink of insanity anyhow. They know they made you and how that happened, but they can't figure out why you are the way you are. They think it is some sort of punishment from God. They think they have done something that displeased God so much that He's paying them back. You know that's true because you always hear parents saying, "What have I ever done to deserve you?" Then they usually say, "I hope God gives you children who treat you the way you treated me. Then you'll be sorry."

And you know, for once, your parents are right. Their thinking is almost on target. You see, they have forgotten how *they* treated *their* folks and how their parents prayed, "I hope God gives you children who treat you the way you treated me. Then you'll be sorry." And God, in His infinite wisdom, did. And you are it. Your parents have forgotten their parents' prayer. They only know that since you turned thirteen you seem to have gone deaf.

"Didn't you hear me tell you to take out the trash? Then why didn't you?"

They also think you have gone blind.

"What's the matter with you? Didn't you see those shoes sitting in the middle of the floor? Why didn't you put them away?"

They also think that you have gotten dumber rather than smarter.

"Why did you do that?"
"I don't know."
"What do you mean, you don't know? Are you stupid or something?"
"I don't know."

Your parents' insecurity is not entirely their fault. No one ever gave them lessons in being parents. If you want to be a licensed (and insured) driver, you have to get a learner's permit. Then you have to take driver's ed. Then you have to practice driving and parallel parking (a skill you'll probably never use again in this day of malls) over and over again. Finally, you have to pass state written and driving tests. Only then are you a licensed driver.

To become a parent all you have to do is . . . um, er, well, you know all you have to do. And there you are with a kid. And the kid keeps growing. No one has given you so much as an owner's guide for the kid much less a book on step-by-step parenting. Situations arise that you don't understand. The child does things you don't understand. If you're like me, they say things you don't understand. And even when you understand, you don't understand. By the time they are teenagers they're driving you crazy.

Even though there is no licensing for parents, there does seem to be a general rule that parents are supposed to make their kids work. This is the reason for their existence. It is their role in life to find garbage for you to take out, homework for you to do, and so on. It is your role to avoid it. That's why you "goof off."

"Why didn't you do your homework?"
"I was just goofin' off."
"What about the housework?"
"Well, I was just goofin' off."

Even though goofin' off is a part of teenage life, you shouldn't major in it. There are lessons to be learned from working. I can't remember any of them just now, but I know there are some. Oh, yes. One thing work teaches you is that you can get most anything done if you want to. Even what seems like a monstrous job. Work sometimes is like eating an elephant. You *do* know how to eat an elephant, don't you? One bite at a time. Eventually you'll finish.

Work is like that. There are jobs we just don't think we'll ever be able to finish. Like writing a term paper—or this book. But, little by little, if we keep at it, the job gets done. Usually to our amazement.

Another thing doing work teaches us is that we may actually find some of it enjoyable. Once we've begun, that is. I always hate cleaning closets or desks. When I do, though, I end up finding the neatest things. Things I'd forgotten I had. Some of them make me laugh; some make me cry. Regardless, I end up having a good time. I've had fun and gotten a clean desk or closet thrown in as a bargain.

Yet a third thing that work can do for us is make us feel good about ourselves. How? Do you remember how you felt the last time you helped someone with work that was troubling them? Like cleaning out an elderly friend's basement. Or raking leaves for an invalid. Or helping your little brother or sister with homework. Felt pretty good, didn't it? Yes, work gives us the opportunity to help others. As God's ambassadors, helping others is what we are supposed to be about.

Life is a mix of things. Hangin', foolin', and goofin' are just three. Work is one more to add to the list. God is our example of how we should work. The Bible tells us He put in a hard six days before taking one to goof off. I don't know about you, but that makes me look forward to Sunday.

So the next time you feel like goofin' off, don't. Spend some time cleaning up your room or taking out the trash. Without being asked to. That'll really drive your folks crazy. And, remember, that's what you're here for.

·· 12 ··

Fun, Fun, Fun

"I can't believe it. Dad said I could take his new BMW cruisin' tonight. When he gave me the keys, he even gave me his gas credit card, the insurance papers, and the registration. That's it, except for the garage door opener. Oh, Dad, you forgot to give me the garage door opener.
Dad.
Dad?
Dad?!
Okay, Dad, real funny.
Dad! ! ! ! ! ! ! ! ! ! !"

I'll bet you thought cruisin' was something new. Well, let me tell you, it's even older than the Beach Boys. Their songs about cruisin' may be the most famous, but there are other, older ones. How about Johnny Bond's "Hot Rod Lincoln" (beautifully redone by Commander Cody and His Lost Planet Airmen). Or Chuck Berry's "No Particular Place to Go." The list could go on and on. Yes, cruisin' has been a part of a teenager's life since long before rock and roll even. Though older folks won't admit it.

Cruisin' is just another teenage rite of passage. Everyone is doing, will do, or has done it. To go cruisin' though, you have to have two things. One is a car. Though this should be obvious, we will talk more about it later. The second thing you need is a place. This place has to be cool or rad or gnarly or whatever the slang word for "really neat" is now. You can't go cruisin' just anywhere. After all, you do have a reputation to consider. You don't want to cruise someplace that is not on the Official

Approved List of Really Neat Cruisin' Places. If you did, and were seen by anyone who is anyone, well, you could kiss your reputation good-bye. Not really. I exaggerated. You'd still have a reputation. Just not the kind you want to have.

When we went cruisin' we cruised Green Gables Drive-In—"on the point, at Central Point." That was where everybody went on Friday and Saturday nights. Greasers with their chopped and channeled '49 Mercuries. The jocks and jockettes in their Ford Mustang convertibles. The rich kids in their MG's and Austin Healy Sprites. And people like me, cruisin' Cool City in our dads' Chevy Bel Airs (four doors and two-tone paint). Everybody from the In-Crowd to the N(erd)-Crowd was there. Round and round Green Gables we'd go. Where we stopped, our parents didn't know. Up and down Mound Street. Out the 3-C Highway. Back around Brown Road. Hot summer nights. Waxed and polished cars. Waxed and polished people. Cold Cokes and greasy fries. What more could a person want? Everybody cruises. It's a part of life. It's a part of growing up.

There are a number of things that have stayed the same about cruisin' since the time Marc Antony first took Cleopatra for a moonlight chariot ride around the local Wendini's. We've already looked at the second. It is important to have the right place to cruise. Let us go back to the first one, which is you have got to have wheels. Let's face facts, it is hard to cruise if you don't have something to cruise in. Now, maybe some guys or girls can walk down to the cruisin' place in town and not look like a joke, but you and I are not them. We need all the help we can get. That means we need a car. If you are one of the few who is so cool you don't need a car to cruise in, pretty soon someone of the opposite sex who has one will offer you a ride. This is not true for the rest of us. We'd look like we'd just missed the National Convention of Bus Riders.

Which brings us to one of the finer points of our first point. (I

74

hope you've gotten all of these points that I've been so carefully pointing out.) That is that just any wheels will not do. A good rule of thumb to keep in mind is that public transportation is not cool. A city bus is not good for cruisin'. Neither is a subway. I'm sorry. They just look bad. Don't even ask about bicycles, unless you're PeeWee Herman. Then it doesn't matter.

A car is a requirement. Any car will do, but Grandma's four-door K-car is to be avoided if possible. The best car to go cruisin' in is, of course, a Ferrari Testarossa. Then it doesn't matter how cool or good-looking you are because no one will really be looking at you anyhow. The car is cool enough and good-looking enough for the whole state. If you have trouble borrowing one (or coming up with the $87,000 to buy your own) you may have to settle for Grandma's K-car.

There are ways to make sure the K-car doesn't kill your evening. First make sure the car is clean, especially on the outside, since that is what everyone will see. The inside will probably be trashed by Pepsi cups, hamburger wrappers, and French fry bags soon anyway. The importance of looking cool cannot be overemphasized. It is what ultimately matters. As my friend Laura says, "It doesn't matter whether you feel good so long as you look good." Words we can all live by. And often do.

Sometimes that's how we treat life. As if what is really important is whether or not we look good. So we spend lots of time getting our outsides ready to impress anyone who sees us. We make sure our clothes are the right ones. We check and check and recheck our faces for the telltale sign of an impending zit attack. Our hair has to be cut, styled, and moussed just so. Inside, however, we may be littered with trash. We may be hateful, hurtful people. We may be mean-spirited and spiteful. We may be good-looking garbage bags—kind of like the new scented ones that are out today. They are colored pretty and smell nice, but inside they are filled with rotting refuse.

Jesus talked to some folks called Pharisees about just this. He wasn't very nice about it, either. He even called them names like whitewashed graveyards, because, while they looked and talked (and probably even smelled) religious, inside they were frauds. Outwardly they did all the right things, but inside they were nasty people. What showed on the external was not a reflection of the internal. What about us. Are we like them?

It may be that we spend too much time getting the outside to look nice. A friend of mine had a great cruisin' car when we were kids. It was a 1930s era Pontiac. He had enough money to fix either the mechanicals or the body. He fixed the body. He had the rust taken off and a great paint job put on. It looked sharp. There was only one problem. It still didn't run right. The thing that would really have made the car a great car had never been attended to. It hadn't been fixed because we wanted to impress the others with how we looked while riding in it. They were impressed all right—until they wanted to go for a ride and it would hardly move. Then our farce was found out.

Life is that way too. We may impress everyone with our looks and clothes and car, but sooner or later we are found out. And there is nothing people like less than a phoney—someone who's masquerading as something they are not. Try to be real, genuine, and good. Let it come from the inside out. God wants that and will help you be the kind whose beauty is not skin-deep, but goes clear to the bone.

The next time you are getting the K-car cleaned up for a night around town looking good, think about that. Remember, "It's not whether you look good. It's whether you *are* good." That's what counts.

•• **13** ••

You Oughta Be in Pictures

"Well, I don't know. We don't normally let our son go to the movies like that. He's so impressionable. But I'll check with Mr. Kruger."

"Honey, is it okay if Freddie goes to see *Bambi Meets Godzilla* with Jason?"

"He can go, but he has to take off that silly hockey mask."

It's dark. Your feet are glued to the floor. You couldn't move no matter what might come your way. A single ray of light coming from behind you is the only illumination in the room other than a dull red glow you can see from the corner of your eye. Weird sounds surrounding you heighten the sense of dread and doom. Suddenly you scream. A madman with a machete lunges from behind a tree at you! Your scream seems multiplied hundreds of times as the air reverberates with horror. You keep screaming and close your eyes, hoping the vision will go away.

A bad dream? No. Real life? Yes and no. You're at the movies.

Of course, horror films like *Dr. Blood in the House of Grisly Axe Murderers* aren't the only cinematic treats offered up. Choices for what kind of movie to go see are tremendous today. You can see a horror film—*Friday the 13th, Part 197—Jason's Great-Grandson Lives!* You can see comedies—*Beverly Hills Cop, 28.* You can indulge in action-dramas—*Rambo, 12.* Sports—*Rocky, 49.*

I'm sure you've noticed by now that every film you go to see has a number behind it. No, they're not the combined IQs of the cast. Except in the case of *Rambo* movies. In all other instances, the number is which sequel it is. One thing Hollywood does, and not very well, is do a good thing to death. Sequels of hits and then sequels of sequels. And each is worse than the first. Instead of getting better, they are stuck in a formula and rely on the same thing over and over.

Crocodile Dundee was great. *Crocodile Dundee—Part 2* was a tad boring. *Star Wars* started out as a one-time movie. It did so well that George Lucas decided it should be the fourth movie of a nine-part series. Good thing for us that numbers 1–3 and 7–9 weren't made, because after the Empire had struck back and the Jedis had their revenge, even Jabba the Hut had had his fill. Sequels are rarely as good as the original. And the further they get from the original, the worse they seem to get. Some of the characters may be the same, but even Luke Skywalker looked almost forty by the time he encountered the Emperor and his dad in *Return of the Jedi.*

Every now and then, though, when you are lined up at the Westland Cinema 45 (45 theaters under one roof, each one holding at least 4,000 people and having a screen the size of the one your dad uses to show the family slides) to pay your $8.50 for a ticket, $2.75 for a small drink, and $4.95 for a bucket of week-old popcorn that even the pigeons in the park won't eat, you will come across a movie that isn't a sequel to anything. It will be fresh and new. It will be funny and sad. It will move you. You'll laugh, you'll cry—you've just kissed $16.20 good-bye. And it will be worth it. The only bad thing is that if it is really good, next year you'll probably suffer through its sequel.

Movies can be wonderful, scary things. Good ones have the power to involve us in their larger-than-life goings-on up on the huge silver screen. Some are so good they become classics. (Con-

trary to popular belief, a classic is not something that's merely old. It has to be good, too. Like me. I am a classic.) Movies, good ones, can suck us in, make us part of their world. Sharon, a friend of mine, watching the classic *Gone With the Wind*, was so captured by the drama and romance of the film, that when Rhett asked, "Miss Scarlett, will you marry me?" a loud "Yes!" was heard throughout the theater. It wasn't Miss Scarlett, though. It was Sharon answering for her. I'm just glad I wasn't with her at the time.

Another friend, Hank, was watching a horror movie where thousands of rats seemed to be streaming off the screen and down the aisles. His wife, sensing he was scared, tried to reassure him by touching his knee lovingly. It worked so well that he screamed and took off down the aisle, sure the rats had him by the leg.

Films can make us cry. They can touch us with their poignancy. Even tough guys have been known to cry at the movies. Though they rarely admit it. As my dad says, "My eyes are just sweating."

Movies are powerful things. They are wonderful in their ability to take us out of our own and place us smack-dab in the middle of the lives of the people up on the screen. What is happening to them seems to be what is happening to us. We bob and weave inside the car as it careens out of control down a steep hill. Someone on the screen starts shooting and we duck. If they scream, we scream. Louder.

That's good—and bad. Movies can help us forget our own mundane existence and live lives of adventure and romance, even if only for an hour and fifty minutes. No longer are we stuck in New Castle, Indiana. Now we're racing down the Amazon with Indiana Jones. We are taken away from taking out the garbage. Instead we are taking out the most beautiful woman in the world. We're not just dreaming of killing the counselors at camp. We're helping Freddie do it.

That's part of the scary, too. Movies aren't real. We can get so involved with them that we run out of the theater screaming or begin answering the characters up on the screen. To escape for a little while is okay, but we need to remain in touch with reality on a regular basis.

Sometimes we run movies in our heads—and we're the stars. We call it daydreaming. Some daydreams are nice; they're fun. But we need to beware that we do not become lost in the fantasyland of our dreams—unless we are using them to urge us on to a new reality, unless we are willing to make our dreams come to pass, no matter how hard that may be.

Movies, and daydreams, can inspire us to do things we've never imagined we could do. God has given us the capacity to dream dreams and go after them. Dreams can keep us alive. If we use them wisely.

What dreams do you have? Lots, I'll bet. You have dreams about the future, close at hand and distant. You dream about life when you finish school. Your boyfriend or girlfriend. Your future husband or wife. Friday night's date. You make yourself your own star and write your own script. You rehearse what you're going to do and say. You try to think of things from every conceivable angle. That's good. Because the more you do that, the clearer the way to making your dream into reality becomes.

Just dreaming doesn't do that. You have to look at your dreams and see what needs to be done to make them happen. You also have to ask yourself if what you are dreaming about is what you really want. If your dream came true, would it be what you desired? Sometimes we don't think about our dreams as if they could become reality. Yet they can. There is a saying that you become what you dream. Is that a good or scary thought?

Movies and dreams have a lot in common. They take us to a

world that we are not in and relieve some of our everydayness. Unlike movies, though, dreams can become reality. God gave you the power to dream dreams and think of great things. God also gave you the power to work at bringing those dreams to pass. You *can* you know. And you should.

•• 14 ••

Shopping

"Tramps like us,
Baby, we were born to shop."

—Brenda Springsteen
from the album
Greetings From Asbury Park Mall

Shopping—one of America's favorite indoor sports. It wasn't always that way. It used to be you had to go outside to shop. You fought the heat and humidity, the rain and snow, the ice and cold. Not anymore. Now, like all major sports, it is an indoor activity, held in a comfortable, climate-controlled environment. In football, it's the stadium. In baseball, it's the field. In basketball, it's the floor. In hockey, it's the arena. In shopping, it's the mall.

And it is no longer a sport dominated by one gender. It was once almost exclusively female, but now many of the major players are men. It used to be that men had their sports and women had theirs. Men played football. Women went shopping. Men played hockey. Women went shopping. Men played basketball. Women went shopping. Men had their sports and women had their sport. But just as girls today are becoming involved in traditionally male sports like soccer and basketball and professional wrestling, so too, are guys popping up shopping. It's only fair in this generation of fighting for male equality.

Now that shopping is being taken seriously as a sport, a whole subculture has developed around it. Categories have been developed. There are several kinds of shopping and shoppers. There is shopping and then there is *shopping*. Amateur and professional. It takes a keen eye to spot the differences. Since they don't sell programs at the mall or have a public address announcer ("Starting at right, shopper is #44, Elizabeth Pierson"), here are some clues so you will be able to tell who is who among shoppers.

First there are those who will go shopping just for the mere thrill of going shopping. They are the amateurs of the sport, though it is here that many pros got their start. For these folks, the joy in shopping is just going. They want to look at everything, find the best bargains, see what's on sale, kill a few hours, and they don't mind if they come home empty-handed. They don't go for any particular reason, they just go. We'll call them "Recreational Shoppers." This is the group I grew up in. Though there may be some who consider me a professional shopper, I know that I really rank at the lowest of the amateur levels.

Recreational Shoppers do not take the sport seriously. They see shopping as just one of many activities they could choose from. It is not seen as an end to itself. These folks do not live to shop, nor do they practice-shop downtown or at strip malls if the real mall has had a power outage or is closed for some other reason. If nothing good is on TV, all of the board games have been played, no money is available to go out to eat or to the movies, and there is absolutely no chance of anybody stopping by for a visit, they go shopping.

My Great-Uncle John was one of these folks. He was my mentor and shopping teacher. A pacesetter in the Men's Lib movement, he led the cause of male shopping long before it was popular. A bachelor all of his life, he shopped constantly. He usually didn't buy anything, maybe a magazine or a book, he just shopped. He used to take us along to teach us the finer points of shopping.

Monday evenings were our time for on-the-job training. We'd load up in his Pontiac Catalina and head for downtown. This was B.M.—Before Malls. We'd park in Lazarus Parking Garage and head through the Lazarus Annex, looking at cameras and sporting equipment, but skipping boring stuff like clothes. Then it was across Town Street, through Lazarus' main store, up the escalators to the fourth floor for books and magazines, fifth floor for records, and sixth floor for toys and pets. We never bought anything. *Yet*. We were "just looking."

Then we'd catch the elevator down to one, duck out through the side doors in Men's Clothing, and head north on High. At Broad Street we crossed over to the east side of High, still heading north. We went through Penney's, bookstores, and anything else that moved us. Then at Long we crossed back to the west side of High and headed south, stopping at the camera stores, candy shops, Planters Peanuts, Woolworth's, and back into Lazarus. The whole loop took about an hour and a half to two hours. Then we usually bought some candy at Lazarus, retrieved the Pontiac, and headed home. All shopped out and nothing to show for it save for the glow in our hearts, knowing we were paving the way for the men shoppers who would follow us.

The next kind of shoppers are "Serious Shoppers." They are serious for two reasons. One, because they shop with a purpose. They go shopping to shop—*for* something. Usually, one thing. Second, they are known as serious because they are not very much fun when shopping. They are not known as Serious Shoppers because they take the sport of shopping seriously. In fact they are much like the Recreational Shoppers in their disregard for the sport's nuances. Unlike the Recreational Shoppers, they see shopping as a nuisance. Something to be endured.

For example, for the serious shopper to go shopping he has to have something to buy. He never just looks around. For him, shopping is work. Hard work. Say the Serious Shopper needs a pair of tennis shoes. He wants a particular kind—Nike Air Bills (Hey, I've got dreams, too). The Serious Shopper will start at Sears and work his way through every store that sells shoes, or looks like it might, gathering prices. He will not stop to look at clothes, jewelry, sporting goods, records, or tapes even if he is right near them. He's on a mission.

"The mission, should you decide to accept it, Mr. Serious Shopper, is to find the lowest price on a pair of Nike Air Bills. If you are caught having a good time, everybody will disavow it because it is so unlike you."

The Serious Shopper will, after comparing prices all over the mall, then purchase the item and head straight home. Mission accomplished.

The final category of shopper is the "Professional, or Shop 'Til You Drop, Shopper." This person is similar to the Recreational Shopper in her love of shopping. That's where the similarity ends. Although the Recreational Shopper enjoys going, he has not put in the sheer amount of hours it takes to turn pro. A recreational type will feel fulfilled after a few hours. The pros go all day and stay all night. They hit every store in the place—at least twice and maybe three times.

The pros don't worry about things like sales or prices. They want to savor the entire retail experience. A pro would not be caught dead in a K mart. It's full price or nothing. Unless of course it is a designer label marked down. Even then it has to be in a mall store. Wal-Mart may be just the place for savings, but not for professional shopping.

Professional Shoppers show up when the first doors open. Usually that's at T. J. Cinnamon's or some such place. There,

munching on an overpriced cinnamon roll and bad coffee, the pros hone their shopping strategies.

"Where can we go to avoid the crowds and have salespeople pay us lots of attention?"

"Who has got the newest fashions in that we can try on?"

"Is there a line at Merle Norman? I'd love to try on cosmetics for a couple or three hours."

"I wonder how many sets of golf clubs we could practice swing in fifteen minutes?"

It's when the doors open that the pros really shine. These folks know their stuff. They visit every nook and cranny of every store. Usually, by closing time, they have just made it out of their first store and are headed for their second. These are the really top-notch pros. For them it is not speed that counts, it's quality time spent in the store.

Yes, shopping can be exciting. If you're doing it. If you're watching it, viewing pro-shopping on SPN ("The All Shopping Network") is even more boring than watching professional bowling. And, as we've pointed out, there are all kinds of shoppers.

Just like there are all kinds of people and types of approaches to life. Some of us look at life recreationally—it's fun and something to do, but let's not get too serious about it. After all, we have enough to do just living it.

Then there are the serious "livers." Every day is hard for them. No joking around, life is serious business. Get done what you have to get done. Don't put anything off. Do it now. Work. Work. Work.

Finally, there are the pros. They look at life as fun and exciting, sometimes serious, and are determined to live it as best they can. The pros want to experience all of life. Not just hit the highlights and call it a day, like the recreational people. Nor with a single-mindedness that shuts out all other possibilities like the serious folks. No, they want to enjoy the highlights but take time out to savor those things that really interest them. They want to ponder the serious, but be open to the thrill of the unexpected.

The pros are the ones who see the sport of life as a combination of discipline and ability. The discipline to do things we should do (even when we don't want to). The ability to go with the flow and trust God to help us.

Jesus was a professional liver. He was serious, to be sure. His mission demanded it. But He had fun, too, like the recreational people. If you read some of His sayings, it's obvious He did a little teasing of the serious folks. And chided the recreational ones for not living life seriously enough.

Yes, Jesus was a pro. And He's our example of how we should live. So, if you're ready to turn pro, use Him as your Mentor and Teacher. And soon you may hear your number called as one of the all-time greats to ever enter Life's Hall of Fame.

·· 15 ··

I Dig Rock and Roll Music

"Rock and Roll is here to stay,
It will never die!"

—Danny and the Juniors, #19 on the Hot 100, 1958

"It's not music, it's a disease."

—Mitch Miller, Columbia Records

If Mitch Miller was right, then it must be a terminal disease, because, as Danny and the Juniors doo-wopped, "rock and roll is here to stay." For over three decades now, rock and roll has been as much a part of teenage life as cruisin', Levi's, and McDonald's. Though plenty of people have tried to kill it off, it will never die.

Everywhere you go, if there's a teenager around, rock and roll will be there. Parents and other adults don't understand this. They know it's true, but they still don't understand. *How can any kid do homework*, they wonder, *with Dr. Zoom and His Sonic Boom blowing their eardrums out?* You know it's possible. You've done it lots of times. And even gotten a C+ or better. So what's the big deal?

That's what the adults want to know. What's the big deal? Why do kids love rock and roll? It's loud, noisy, overblown, and you can't understand most of the words. That's why you like it, right? You like it because it is loud, noisy, and overblown. And who cares that you can't understand the words? All that's important is that it sounds good and has enough backbeat to shake all of the leaves off Mr. Lee's trees if you turn the Sanyo up loud enough.

Most people, even those who are not teenagers, like music. Old folks do. Real old folks, like your parents, do. Even little kids do. But compared to rock and roll, their music is just music. Your music, on the other hand, is an expression of your life and life-style. It helps define who you are and where you are going. Besides, it's got a great beat and it's easy to dance to.

"I'll give it an 85, Dick."
"Thanks, Lisa, now back to 'Bandstand.' "

Your teenage years are special and unique ones. And one way to keep them special and unique is to shut your parents out. Who wants them around? They're not much fun. Besides, just because they want to know everything that is going on in your life is no reason they should. And what better way to shut them out than by listening to rock and roll. You know there's no way that what you consider rock and roll and what they think of when they hear those words are anywhere close to the same idea. They think of Chuck Berry, Elvis, Buddy Holly and the Crickets. Or if they are not *real* old—the Beatles (a group Paul McCartney used to be in) or the Hollies or the Association. You think of Tiffany or Michael Jackson or Huey Lewis and the News. There's no comparison. Even if you ask them to listen to rock and roll with you, and chances are they won't want to, you'll be tuning in "WAPL—The Rock of New York" and they'll be thinking of "Stanley Banker's All-Night, All-Request Golden Oldies Show" ("And now, Johnny Mathis with 'Chances Are' ").

If you listen to rock very much (and if you are a real teenager, that's the only way you listen to it), you probably won't have to see your folks very much. Only when it's feeding time or you have to go to school or something. And that's part of the point of being a teenager—not being around your parents. They may complain but really wouldn't want it any other way. When you are not eating, you can lock yourself in your room with Tina Turner or George Michael and make the world go away.

If you do have to be around your parents, you can still take rock and roll with you and stay detached from the situation. How? You know the answer. You wear your Walkman. Put the earphones on. Keep them on all through supper. This is guaranteed to drive parents crazy. It also comes in handy if you want to fool them into thinking you're someone else. All you have to do is take off your stereo. Chances are they won't have seen you without your headphones for so long, they won't recognize you.

"Say, honey, who's the boy with the ears? He's not our son, is he?"

"No, dear, it couldn't be. Our boy Timothy lost his ears somewhere around the seventh grade."

Yes, rock and roll is a way to be in your own little world. A world made up of three-minute romances, horror stories, car races, and most anything else you can imagine. Of course, if you have MTV, you won't need to imagine much, because instead of using your brain to fill in the pictures that go along with the lyrics, music videos do it for you.

Rock and roll does create its own world. It has the power to move us from the mundane to the marvelous and back again. Music has the ability to bring excitement to our boring lives. Unfortunately, it sometimes does that by ultimately causing us to sacrifice other life experiences.

Life is—or can be—a lot of fun, but only if we live it. If we spend all our time cooped up in our rooms listening to tunes, we are missing the world outside our rooms. And believe me, there is a lot of world outside. There are things to do and people to see. There are new places to go and new things to experience. Just think, if you took your headphones off, you might actually hear something that didn't have a backbeat and still sounded pretty good. Like your mother calling to let you know she baked your favorite cake or something like that. If you keep your phones on, your little brother will eat all of the cake before you even know about it.

Yes, life is for living. But not always to a sound track. I think we've watched so many videos and movies that we think there has to be music for every situation. We have scary music for horror movies, dramatic music for action flicks, and sweet, sappy stuff for love stories. If it's that way on the silver screen, we want it that way in life. So we lock ourselves up with rock and roll. What that means is that we sometimes miss the music that exists in the world around us. Music that is always there, but we've grown tone-deaf from having the volume set on high all the time.

I'm not saying you shouldn't listen to rock and roll. I do. But there are times when it wouldn't hurt to put it aside for a while. In fact, it might help. You might then be able to hear things you haven't heard for some time. Like a bird singing. Or someone laughing. Or even God talking to you.

It's hard to hear when there is always something going on in your ear. So take a break. Get quiet. Listen to the music all around you. It's music that often comes from the most remarkable place of all—God's creation. Stop and take a listen.

Part III

Johnny Bee's Sophisticated System
for Dating Members of
the Opposite Sex

·· **16** ··

Lesson 1: Introduction to Dating

Dating—the art of going out with someone, dressing up nicer than you usually do, spending money, and acting like you are having a fun, relaxing time when all the while you are so nervous you feel like throwing up.

Going on a date is a lot like going to a football game. That ought to excite most of you female readers, since there is nothing like spending hours sitting shivering on cold metal bleachers, watching a bunch of guys beat each other up. Yet, there are similarities between football and dating. The big date is like the big game in profound yet subtle ways. There are pre-date (game) rituals that must be performed and events happen in patterns (quarters). Then the gun finally sounds—the date (game) is over. We'll explore each of these as we progress through "Johnny Bee's Sophisticated System for Dating Members of the Opposite Sex" (in my opinion, the only kind to date). If you carefully complete all the correct (do not use the bad ideas) steps that follow, I guarantee that you will be the success with the opposite sex that I am. Okay, okay, you should do a lot better than I have. Learn from my mistakes.

Warning: These lessons may be hazardous to your love life. Please take them in the order they are presented.

Though you may feel you are sufficiently advanced in the science of dating, you skip any of these at your own risk. The management assumes no responsibility for a bad date. Follow the instructions carefully and you'll wear your diploma with pride. You may even get a date. Skim the material and you could end up on a bad date. It will be your own fault and all of your friends will laugh at you. I will, too. And probably say, "I told you so," because I am an adult and I'm allowed to. Your money will not be cheerfully refunded.

Step 1: Getting Your Own Date

The most important pre-date ritual is that of asking someone out. By yourself. With no help from friends. Almost anyone has the chance to go out on a date if his or her friends arrange it. What we are talking about here is getting your own date. Solo. Well, maybe with some instructions written on the inside of your wrist (if it works in Algebra, it will work here). If you don't ask someone out, you needn't bother worrying about how the game, I mean date, is going to go. This should be obvious. Once you have familiarized yourself with this point, you may proceed with step 1.

Asking someone out takes lots of planning. That is because if you do not have the date planned before you ask you may as well forget it. For some strange reason (unknown to all except to early Egyptians, whose Mummy taught them all about it) prospective dates like to have some clue as to what they might be going to do if they go out with you. I realize that the mere pleasure of being in your company for two to three or ten hours should be enough. Some folks just can't be pleased. They want to know what you are going to do. This requires planning.

Back when I was first dating (and humans spoke in grunts, groans, and whistles—a lot like Phys Ed class today), asking someone out was the sole privilege of male members of the species. If you were a boy it gave you something to dread all through elementary and junior high school. You heard horror stories of guys who blew it big while asking a girl out. They were never seen again. Swallowed by the black hole of dating. That's a real confidence builder, let me assure you. In the olden days, when the only Coke there was was soda pop and Miami Vice was an illegal bingo game on the beach, if a girl dared to ask a guy out, it was for Sadie Hawkins Day (a quaint ritual of the olden days) or a "Turnabout Dance." If a girl asked a guy out at any other time, then she was "one of those kind of girls." Whatever "one of those kind of girls" was. I don't know. We were never told. Specifics were left out. The tone of Mom's voice said it all. And it must have been really bad. Whatever it was, mothers always warned sons about *those kind of girls* and prayed their daughters would not become one. It's scary to think how many young women during the fifties and sixties almost became *those kind of girls* just because they accidentally phoned a fella and hinted around for a date. I guess since they didn't come right out and ask the guy to the movies, it was okay. All of those moms' prayers and threats (and locking Connie in the closet) must have worked. I know I was never asked out by a girl.

Times have changed, though, and girls are always calling my house. Of course, they all want to ask Ben out, not me.

In this liberated age, a girl asking for a date can be as thoroughly humiliated as a guy. I think this is a giant step for womankind. Now *they* can get the pre-phone-call jitters. *They* can lie awake nights on end rehearsing how to ask and fearing the rejection that is sure to follow. America—what a country. What other place assures all its citizens, male or female, of their rights to life, liberty, and the pursuit of a Friday night date?

Now you see that the possibilities for a misstep are almost endless. Stress like this is the best invention for staying awake since No Doz. Of course, if you keep stressed out like this for weeks before the date, you'll probably fall asleep while you're on it. So, to keep Pre-Date Stress (also known as PDS) at a minimum, preplan your entire date.

When planning make sure what you're going to do on the date will be things a fairly normal person would want to do. Do not rely on your or any of your friends' judgment in this matter—you may not qualify as "fairly normal." This is too important an area to mess up. You want your dates to have fun. If they don't have fun with you, they will with someone else. Maybe someone else they met while on a date with you.

A good way to find out what your prospective date might like to do is to ask his or her best friend what they think your date might like to do. After all, this person is really, really, really close to your date and might even remember what he or she likes and doesn't like. While this approach sounds safe, even it has its dangers. The most notable one is that they warn the prospective date so she or he can have excuses lined up before you even get a chance to call and embarrass yourself.

"Gee, Dan, I'd really like to go, but I have to groom my cat that night."
"But that's what you said last week, Jo."

Another danger is that they will lie to you. They might do this for one of two reasons. The first is they don't want their friend going out with you. The second is they just like humiliating people.

"No, I would not be interested in going to the Museum of Antique Dental Appliances with you! Where did you ever come up with a dumb idea like that? Oh, right. Like I'm sure my best friend Jenny would suggest something stupid like that."

Of course, there is the chance they might like you, but this happens so rarely as to be almost impossible. So, after thinking it over, and writing it down, I guess asking their best friend is not a good idea. Actually, I would suggest you avoid even talking to their friends. The possible bad far outweighs the good.

I do want to be helpful, though. And I know that what I have told you so far has been. However, it has been pretty basic stuff. Now we are going to go into the deep realms of dating. We'll set off boldly where no human has gone before. Excuse me. I guess I got carried away. You will need to pay close attention from this point as we leave basic and move to advanced.

The first advanced point is this—the differences between a good date and a bad date are often very subtle. That is why preparation is so important. Even saying something as innocent as "Do you want to go out to eat Friday night?" leaves you wide open to possible disaster. That's because you may be thinking, *Kentucky Fried Chicken*, and he or she's thinking *Max's Chez Reese*. Think. Plan. Think. Plan. Think. Plan. These, and following the steps below, ensure you a good date.

For Guys Asking Out Girls

Question: Would you like to go out to eat at . . .
Good: the best seafood place in town?
Bad: White Castle?

Question: Would you like to go see . . .
Good: a really sensitive play that the university's theater department is performing this month?
Bad: Roller Derby at the Highland County Fairgrounds?

Question: Would you like to . . .
Good: go with me while I do my weekly volunteer work at the humane society, getting some of the unwanted, unloved puppies ready for adoption?

Bad: go with me while I toilet paper David Hosea's house?

For Girls Asking Out Guys

Question: Would you like to go out to eat at . . .
Good: White Castle?
Bad: the best seafood place in town?

Question: Would you like to go see . . .
Good: Roller Derby at the Highland County Fairgrounds?
Bad: a really sensitive play that the university's theater department is performing this month?

Question: Would you like to . . .
Good: go with me while I toilet paper Charlotte Smeken's house?
Bad: go with me while I do my weekly volunteer work at the humane society, getting some of the unwanted, unloved puppies ready for adoption?

While all of the above are generalizations, they are a pretty good rule of thumb. You are generally safe, if a guy, to ask a girl out to eat at someplace nice, to do something nice, or go see something nice. Niceness and sensitivity count. Girls like that. They will tell other girls that you are sensitive and nice. Then other girls will want to go out with you because you are sensitive and nice. And you can dump the one you were going with.

You are safe, if a girl, if you ask a guy out to eat most anything, do most anything, or see most anything. Discrimination is not a male specialty, contrary to the images that Phil Donahue, Geraldo Rivera, and Alan Alda try to project. For all the work that our mothers have done on us, most of us guys don't care what we do. That's why if you ask a guy what he wants to do, he'll usually shrug and say, "I don't care." Usually, he doesn't. The other times, he does, but knows that saying "I don't care" really makes females go crazy with anger and this is great fun for a guy. "But I *want* you to care!" she cries.

So, an important pre-date ritual is to plan, plan, plan. And don't worry about things going wrong. They will.

Planning is a good thing to do in life, too. Though we can overplan at times to the point of inflexibility, we need to have a general idea of where we are going. That will help us know when we've gotten there.

God wants to help us with all this planning. Sometimes we seem to think that God's plans for us can't be any fun—like He wants us to be missionaries to San Timonious and get malaria and have no money and get sick and die. Or just plain hate it. Chances are that's just not so. As I've said earlier, God wants the best for us. And the best for us also means that we enjoy where life takes us. Just like a good date requires planning, so does a good life. Think about the things you like to do. And want to do. How do you want your life to turn out?

I believe that God has very special plans for all of us. Included in the plan for you is a life better than you can even imagine for yourself. We need to take time to include God in our planning for life. He really knows what makes a good date, ah, life, for every girl or guy.

•• 17 ••

Lesson 2: Asking Her / Him / It Out

Here comes Nathaniel. He is sooo good-looking. I'd give anything to go out with him. I wish, I wish, I wish . . . Oh! He's coming this way.

"Say, Cathy, how would you like to go out with me Friday night?"

Okay, now be cool. Just because this is what you've always dreamed of doesn't mean you should be nervous. Just say, Why, Nathaniel, I'd love to.

"Uh, em, ur, duh,—aaarrrgghh!!!!!"

"Is that a yes or a no?"

Okay, so now you've made your plans. You've done all your preplanning, called AAA for a road map, saved all of your allowance to pay for the big night. Now comes another hard part. (If you have figured out that dating has lots of hard parts, you'll be okay. If you think it is going to be easy . . . well, just skip to the end of the book. Your date probably already has.) Now you have to

A. Invite her to go out to dinner and see a play after you've finished up your volunteer time at the humane society.

B. Invite him to hit White Castle, see Roller Derby, and toilet paper Charlotte Smeken's house on the way home.

Just how to ask someone out is of the utmost importance. There are only a few ways to do this: in person, over the phone, by registered letter, or by bribing a friend to do it for you. (The drawback to this last choice is that if the date says yes your friend may "forget" to tell you and take her out himself.) Which way you choose depends on how strong your ego is. If you don't know what ego strength is, chances are you don't have any, you big dummy. Did it hurt when I called you "big dummy"? If so, your ego strength is fragile. Forget about asking someone out for a date. Just lock yourself in your room until graduation comes or your zits disappear (whichever comes first) or till you've moved to a town where nobody knows you. Try then. If you said, "Who're you calling a big dummy, you big dummy?" then your ego strength is okay and you will probably survive asking someone out. The key word there is *probably*. In dating, as in all of life, there are no guarantees—and those that do exist only last twelve months or 12,000 miles, whichever comes first. Which has nothing to do with dating, unless you live in Alaska or Kansas, where it takes twelve months or 12,000 miles just to reach your date's house.

The best way to ask someone out is face-to-face. The main benefit here is that you get it over with quickly. You know right then and there whether she really wants to go out with you or not. The facial expressions are a dead giveaway. On the phone she can lie through their teeth. You can't tell that while she's saying, "I'd love to, but . . ." she's simultaneously sticking a finger down her throat and pretending to gag. If someone does that in person, it is a good clue that this person is not taking your invitation too seriously. And if *he* says, "Yes!!!" just the chance to watch his face light up with joy at being asked should be reward enough.

Asking someone out face-to-face is also the hardest. It is one thing to have someone laugh at you over the phone and quite another to be guffawed at right to your face. In person. In the hall at school. Surrounded by all your friends. And enemies. That's hard to recover from. So, if you can ask someone out face-to-face, get rejected, and come back with something witty like

"Oh, yeah, well, um, uh . . ." and not show your disappointment, then ask face-to-face. Otherwise, use the telephone.

Which brings us to method number two. The telephone. Telefon. Telephono. Ma Bell. The phone and dating go together like pizza and pepperoni, cherry and Coke, ham hocks and grits. Dating is what the phone was made for. Do you think Alexander Graham Bell came up with the idea just to ease communication? No way. He wanted to call up some girl for a date. So he invented the phone. And teenagers (and others possessing low ego strength) have been grateful ever since.

Using the phone to get a date has distinct advantages. You can't see her make faces as she turns you down. You can pretend you've gotten a bad connection and say something like, "No, I didn't ask you for a *date after* school. I just called to ask if you'd ever been *late to* school. Must have gotten a bad line."

To make this more realistic, you need to turn the dial or punch the buttons occasionally to provide the proper static.

As easy as using the phone to arrange a rendezvous is (or "tele-dating" as we here at the Johnny Bee School of Dating call it), there are certain things not to do on the phone while asking for a date. These are listed below for your information.

Phone No-No's

Never belch into the receiver.

Try to keep this in mind.

For your help and edification, two sample phone calls follow. For the sake of clarity we will call one "Right" and one "Wrong."

Right

The date is for Friday evening. The call is made on Monday after school.

"Hello, Mrs. Sweitzer. This is Robert Manners. May I please speak with Amy Jo? Thank you. Hi, Amy Jo, this is Robert from school. Would you care to join me this Friday evening for dinner at Max's Chez Reese and a film? Grand, I'll pick you up at 6:30. Tell your lovely mother good-bye for me. See you at school tomorrow."

Wrong

The date is for Friday evening. The call is made Friday evening at 5:30.

"Hi, who is this? Oh, yeah, is Mary Ann there? No, I don't wanna speak to her, I just wanta know if she's there. Of course, I'm kidding. Can I talk with her, if ya don't mind? Hey, M.A., I didn't have nothing to do and wanted to know if you wanna grab some burgers and roller derby over at the fairgrounds? Oh, yeah, and I'm going to teepee Evan's house on the way back, too.

"Whadaya mean ya gotta warsh your hair tonight?"

While the wrong one may work if you are calling one of your friends, it will not make an impression on "that special someone." Well, it will, but not the impression you want to make.

So, follow Johnny Bee's Systematic Easy Steps to Success with the Opposite Sex and you, too, will be in date heaven. All you have to do is do it right.

That's important, doing things right. And not just in dating. When we do something right, it gives us a good feeling. There's a rightness about it. You know what I mean. It just *feels* right. I know that's a lot of "rights" but think about it for a few minutes.

I'm not necessarily talking about doing the "right thing" in a moral sense. In some situations there is no "right thing" that heads the list of choices. But in almost every situation there is a solution that, in our heart of hearts, feels the best. And maybe "best" is another way to say "right."

When you look at life—whether it's your date life or just the plain old life you live every day—you need to look for the best. What is best for you, your friends, family, school, or work? What's fair? What's just? What is right?

You won't always do the right thing. No one does. Not even our 83-year-old grandmas. And the 83-year-old grandmas are the first to admit it. But we need to try. We have to give everything in life our best shot. Sometimes our aim will be off. That's okay. Other times, other people will say we didn't give it our best. That can be okay too, if we—and God—know that we have. We may find ourselves accused of things we didn't do, things that were not the best. If we know deep down inside that we have done our best, and that God has been with us all along, then what the others say really doesn't matter. Even when it feels like it does. For their words go away, but our own actions can haunt us forever.

So do what feels right in your heart of hearts, the deepest part of your soul. The benefits will far outweigh the costs. God wants us to do things right and will help us if we just ask. Right on!

Lesson 3: Pre-Date Checklist

"Let's see, I don't think I've forgotten anything. I've got the car keys, concert tickets, dinner reservations, a cute card to give her, and flowers. Yep, that's it . . . except for one thing. Hey, Mom, do you remember who it was I asked out?"

Well, the hard part is over. You've preplanned, planned, and replanned what to do on your big date. More than that, you've even gotten someone to go with you. And you've done it all yourself. You didn't buy someone else's plans to a successful past date (if you need some, call me at 1-800-WANA-DATE). You didn't bribe anyone to ask for you. It was hard, but you did it. Now comes your reward—a real date. It's got to be smooth sailing from here on out, right? "The hard part is over." That's what you think. If you don't keep following (and hopefully memorizing; there will be a test later) these lessons, the really hard stuff might be just beginning. But lucky for you, there is the following handy-dandy Pre-Date Checklist. Use it and be a wildly successful dater. Kids from miles around will look at you and say, "Gee, Ashley, I wish I could date like that (sigh)." Only *you* will know that you owe much of your success to the Pre-Date Checklist that was included as part of the tuition in Johnny Bee's Sophisticated System for Dating Members of the Opposite Sex.

Other would-be daters (like you used to be, before this course) make serious mistakes before they even go out on the date. Many of these errors are costly and could scar both the dater and datee for years. Generations even. In most cases these mistakes could have been avoided. If these people had only had access to the knowledge that is about to be imparted to you. Please, do not share this with anyone who is not enrolled in the course. Without all of the other training, it may just be too much for them. A kind of social overload. And besides, you don't want them learning the techniques that made you and me so cool, do you? They might come and take our girlfriend or boyfriend. If they want to learn it, make them buy the book. (Do not—I repeat, *do not*—think you can sell them yours. This will not work. I have kept track of who has this information and if you even think about giving it away I will come over to your house and make your life miserable. Just like I do to the kids at my house. Ahem. Back to the lesson.)

Pre-Date Checklist

General [For Either Gender]

___ Transportation arranged (preferably neither parent driving nor public transportation).
___ Shower (take one).
___ Brush teeth. With toothpaste. Use toothbrush.
___ Gargle. Try to use mouthwash. A mixture of 1 part toothpaste to 49,000 parts water will do in a pinch.
___ Wash hair. With shampoo. Cream rinse optional.
___ Trim fingernails and toenails.
___ Shave (if or wherever necessary).
___ Comb hair(s).
___ Clean underwear (as Mother says, "You might be in an accident and you don't want people to think your mother

couldn't keep you in clean underwear, now do you?" Also known as a mother's worst fear. Not that you'll be in an accident, but that you'll be in an accident wearing dirty underwear.)

___ Use deodorant. Do not scrimp (you will probably sweat enough to fill five bathtubs).

___ Cologne yourself. Do not overdo this.

___ Clean clothes appropriate for date (i.e., formal wear for prom, Levi's for miniature golf, and coveralls and Farm Bureau cap for Tractor Pull night).

___ Buttons in proper buttonholes.

___ Zippers zipped and locked.

___ Breath mints. Lots of them.

___ Shoelaces tied (dress shoes) or untied (tennis shoes or loafers).

___ Money to pay for date (if dater).

___ Money for cab fare home (if datee).

These things will not guarantee that your date will be successful. But they will at least help you get off to a good start. You will arrive at your date's home reasonably well-groomed, clean, and nice-smelling. You will have your clothes on in all the right places and won't have to worry about whether or not you buttoned, zipped, and tied everything. A quick glance at the pre-date checklist and you'll know whether you are in good shape or in danger of killing her father with your breath because you forgot to gargle.

Showing up in reasonably good shape (you don't want to look too perfect; after all, you're a teenager, not a Vulcan) is a good move. Your date will like it and it goes over well with parents. Believe me, you want the parents on your side. As you'll see in the next chapter.

In life, too, things go a lot easier and you have a better chance of being successful if you use a checklist. Most of us hate checklists and certainly don't want to use one every day. But often, if we don't check our lists, we forget to do things that are important, helpful, or save us from a lot of embarrassment. Besides, we are always meaning to do something, but "I forgot." A checklist helps us to not forget.

Below are some of the things that you should check daily during your date with life.

Johnny Bee's Sophisticated System for Daily Living
Pre-Day Checklist

__ Talked with God.
__ Read Bible.
__ Talked with God.
__ Talked with friends and others about God.
__ Talked with God.
__ Attended Sunday school and worship.
__ Talked with God.
__ Went to Youth Group.
__ Talked with God.
__ Talked with God.
__ Talked with God.

I guess by now you can see which one of the things on the checklist I think is most important. You need to check (and more than once a day) that you have spent time talking to God. A special time or format is not needed. God is as near as your heartbeat. Use your checklist to make sure you haven't forgotten to talk with Someone who wants to be the best friend you've ever had.

No checklist can ensure that everything will go as you plan. Not the pre-date one; not even the pre-day one. But, we can all do things that make our lives easier. We decide the outcome of our lives, and we need to do the things that make for the kind of life we want. If we want to live godly lives then we need to spend

113

time with God and do the things that help us learn about God.

So the next time you're going on a date, use the Pre-Date Checklist. And the next time you want help with your life (which should be daily), look at the Pre-Day Checklist. It's your life. Check it out.

19

Lesson 4: Dealing With Your Date's Parents

"So you are the young man who's taking my little Jennifer out tonight. That's nice. Now before you go, let me see your driver's license, proof of car insurance, an affadavit of clean health from your doctor, two references, a statement of your last year's earnings. . . ."

Something scarier than all of the *Friday the 13th, Hallowe'en,* and Pee Wee Herman movies rolled into one is going to happen to you on your date. No, I don't mean your grandma is going along as a chaperone. This is worse than that. The most terrifying moment on a date is meeting your date's parents. You may not be worried if you already know them. You should be. It's just not the same anymore. Parents who have been friendly to you when you were just some kid they knew look at you in a completely different way when you are a prospective date for their little girl or boy.

From the nice, intelligent, well-groomed and mannered individual that they always thought you were, you have suddenly turned into someone who makes Jack the Ripper seem like just a man who played with a pocketknife. From the time you ask their child (I know you don't think of yourself as a child, but your parents always will. My grandmother, in her eighties, always says to my father, in his late fifties, as he leaves the house, "Now, Jack, you look when you cross that street. The cars come awfully fast." It must be good advice, though, because he hasn't been hit yet and has been crossing that street almost fifty years) to go out on a date, you may notice someone following you. Parents have been known to hire private eyes or call in the FBI (Federal Boy Investigators) to check out the menace to their offspring. And that's the parents who *know* you. Trust me, I've been there.

If they don't know you, it's even worse. You will probably have to fill out an application like the one below.

Prospective Date Information

The information gathered on this sheet will be held in the strictest confidence. Unless of course, we feel like sharing it with the world and "60 Minutes."

Name_____ Nickname_____

Side of town: Good_____ Okay_____ Bad_____ Worse than bad_____

Father's salary_____ Mother's salary_____ Your salary_____

Childhood diseases_____ Current diseases_____

Zits_____ Braces_____ Other medical_____

Car (make, model, and year)_____ Yours or parents_____

Proposed date (schedule and locations)_____

_____

Names & phone numbers of three references:_____

_____

It is important that you complete this form correctly. Answer all the questions truthfully. Parents, as you know, have ways of finding out if you are lying. If you want to go on a date with their child, be honest. It's the best policy (unless of course you are a veteran between the ages 25–55 and would like group insurance. Then watch late-night TV because they have lots of policies for you).

Having told you to be truthful, which is important, I need to let you know how you can use this form to your benefit. If I don't help you, you may be too truthful and blow the whole thing. Though I am breaking the "Code of Silence" (which is rigorously enforced by the National Parents Association) by giving you this information, I do occasionally have memory flashbacks to my teenage years. I could have used this type of help. All I ask is that you pay attention and don't tell anyone where you got this stuff.

All the questions are important. Some are a little trickier than others. Carefully read the material below and you'll do okay. As indicated, some of these questions deserve special attention. Take your time; do not rush. The date you save may be your own.

Name. This is not a trick question. Don't act too silly here. Parents, being old and in pain a lot of the time, don't like silly. Put down your real name. Even if you hate it.

Nickname. This is very serious. Parents put a lot of stock in nicknames. Fathers are not prone to let their daughters go out with guys nicknamed "Stud" or "Snake." Likewise, mothers don't like their sons dating a girl who's known as "Wild Thing."

Side of town. Parents want their kids to do as well or better than they did. Therefore, they trust (not that any parent *really* trusts any teenager) teenagers who come from their own social class or those above them. It is always smart, from a parent's standpoint, to stay at your own level or go higher.

Salaries. It's okay for your folks to make more than your date's folks—so long as it is not too much more. It is never okay for you to make more than your date's folks.

Diseases. Parents do not want their kids going out with former typhoid carriers or anyone who has anything at the time. Do not show up for your date wearing a surgical mask or taking lots of medication.

Zits and Braces. These are normal and it's okay to have these. Just not too many. If under "Nickname" you wrote *Pizza Face,* don't bother to fill out the rest of the form. It won't matter.

Car. Should be reasonably new and boring—"1986 Dodge Omni 4-door" is the kind of thing parents like to see written in this space. Real old and boring is okay, too. A 1953 Nash Ambassador like my first car was very okay. A brand-new Mustang 5.0 GT is not good. Fast cars driven by teenagers scare parents. Some cars are acceptable if owned by the parents. Your parents' new Lincoln Town Car is okay. Your new Lincoln Town Car is not. If you have any questions see "Salaries."

Proposed schedule and locations of date. This is very important. Fudge a little here if you have to. Don't lie, just be creative. For example, don't write *Roller Derby.* Write *Athletic event.* Don't write *Cruisin'.* Write *Visit historic sites.* Don't write *10:30.* Write *10 or so.* It is important to give yourself some leeway. Be specifically general. Do not leave too much room or the parents' fertile imaginations will fill in the blanks.

References. This is extremely important. Good references to use are grandparents (if they love you and think you're an angel. And what grandparent doesn't?), your dad's boss (if you've been especially polite to him or her), neighbors (if you shovel their snow or cut their grass and haven't teepeed their house lately), and your pastor (if he has seen you in church since last Christmas or Easter). Never use the leader of the local Hell's Angels, your best friend or any other teenager, or your old boyfriend or girlfriend (they can tell things about you, whether true or not, to ensure you never get another date with anyone, anywhere).

Of course, what all this shows is that parents really do care. They want the best for their kids. That's you. Sometimes you think they go overboard. Sometimes they do. But only sometimes. Okay, they go overboard lots of times. But the important thing to remember is *why* they do. It's because they love you.

You may not believe it at the time, but it's true. There are times when they even like you. They want the best for you and try to keep you from getting hurt. I know you'll find this hard to swallow, but your parents were teenagers once. They had boyfriends and girlfriends. They went on dates. They had their hearts broken. Broken so bad that they don't want that to happen to you. So, at times they get overprotective.

God is like a parent to us, too. Sometimes like a father, sometimes like a mother. Always watching out for us. Not watching us to see if we make a mistake or something, but watching out for us. Wanting to warn us of possible dangers and hardships ahead. That's because God wants the best for us. So He watches over us. For our own good.

Yes, there are times when we wonder if our parents' sole purpose in life is to make us miserable. It is sometimes. But most of the time they do what they do because they love us so much. God is the same way. Our Heavenly Parent loves us even more than our earthly ones. Who can go wrong with that much love? Relax, enjoy, and thank God for it. I do.

•• 20 ••

Lesson 5: Waiting for Your Date

"Don't you think you should finish getting ready and go meet your date? He's been waiting for two and a half hours now."

"Well, Mom, you said I shouldn't appear overanxious."

"That's true, but you should appear."

It's here. It's come. Time to go on your date. You've preplanned, you've asked your date to go, you've run through your pre-date checklist, and even weathered meeting your date's parents. You've done it all. And everything you have done so far has prepared you for this moment. Well, *almost* prepared you. As much as I hate to say it, no amount of preplanning and preparation takes into account the unexpected. If anything unanticipated can crop up, it will. Count on something you hadn't planned on happening. Because it will. This has nothing to do with the rest of this chapter. It's just a disclaimer, like the one the Surgeon General puts on cigarette packets.

Come to think of it, maybe a date should come with a disclaimer. You know, something like

"**Caution:** The date you are going on will not be anything like what you imagined while planning it."

That would be truth in advertising. Dates, no matter how well planned, never turn out exactly the way you thought they would. Or wish they would. Or should.

Let's get back to our main topic—it's time to go. If you are going on a date, you are one of two things. They are the only choices available to you, unless your family still insists on chaperones. Then you could be one of those for your brother's or sister's date. Chances are, though, that you are either the "pickup-ee" or the "pickup-er." It is better to be the former. 'Tis a far far better thing to be picked up than to pick up. It's a lot less work. You don't have to arrange transportation, be on time, or any of that kind of stuff. And, after all, you already know your parents, so they won't be grilling *you*. Your date will have to suffer through that.

Plus if you are being picked up it is okay to be fashionably late, to make an entrance. This gives you a chance to do those little last-minute things like putting together a matching outfit or taking a shower. These are things some of us never seem to be able to get done on time. No matter how hard we try. It is okay to make someone who came to get you wait downstairs. It is not so good to be late picking someone up. All in all, try to arrange to be the one picked up.

If you can't set it up that way, and you find you are doing the picking up, you have the harder job. You want, no, have, to be on time. Don't ever be late. It infuriates your date and says something supposedly important about your character to the parents. I'm not sure what it is, but parents seem to have the crazy notion that punctuality is a good character trait. I'm sure that if Attila the Hun had been punctual picking up dates, the parents would have loved him even if he did sack Western civilization. I know it doesn't make sense, but trust me on this. Either be on time by every clock in town (and make sure there is only one time zone in town, not two, like Union City, Indiana, and Union City, Ohio) or be early. But not too early. Five minutes early is good. Twenty-five is not. After all, if you show up too early, and your date has graduated from Pierson's

Procrastination Parlay, there's no way you'll get out of there anywhere close to on time. That's that much more time you have to spend with your date's folks. Feeling awkward.

If you are the picker-upper you will have to make conversation with the parents, little brothers and sisters, grandparents, neighbors, and anyone else who happens to stop by. This is another part of the test, like punctuality. Your date will hardly ever be waiting breathlessly at the door for you (*see* "fashionably late" above). It's never good to sit out front, honk the horn, and play your radio really loud while waiting, either. You have to go in the house. The best way to prepare for this encounter is to keep a few simple rules in mind.

Rules for Talking With Parents

1. Don't say anything stupid.

That about covers it. You want me to tell you what's not stupid? Well, dealing with parents is tricky, and though I'm not really sure I should help you out that much, I will. Here are three ways to successfully speak with parents.

1. Be polite. Parents love teenagers who are polite. That's because they are so rare. Just in case you have forgotten, here is a brief politeness phrase list.

Yes, sir.
No thank you, ma'am.
Please.
Pardon me.
You are quite welcome.
You've been most kind.
Thank you.
Please.
Sir.
Ma'am.

Try to insert the last four into your part of the conversation whenever possible.

2. *Compliment them.* Try not to sound like Eddie Haskell on "Leave It to Beaver." "Gee, Mrs. Cleaver, that's a lovely dress you're wearing" is not a very good line. People like to be complimented but generally want it to sound like you mean it. Even if you don't. Practice being sincere. Trust me on this; if you can fake sincerity you've got it made.

3. *Agree with them.* If they ask you what you think about sports, politics, or nuclear physics, find out what they think before you answer. You can do that by saying, "Well, sir, I'm not really sure my feeble mind is capable of understanding all the ramifications of the 3-1-1 basketball defense. How do you feel about it?" Then parrot back what they just said. It confirms in their minds that you are a good kid, because you remind them of themselves.

You may think that instead of taking the risk of saying something stupid you won't say anything. *I'll just sit here and keep my mouth shut. That should be safe.* Wrong. This is not good either. Think about it. If you sit there you have to do something with your hands. If you sit there with them folded in your lap, they might think you just died. No kid can sit that still. If you're just sitting there, watch your hands. They start moving on their own—often without your even being aware of it—until the fool things have gone and done something stupid. Like you're sitting there in silence with your date's parents, and your hand slowly makes its way up to your face. And you aren't even aware of it. Until you wonder where your index finger is and you find it up your left nostril. So make conversation. You need to talk at least enough to keep yourself from doing anything stupid.

You can say something stupid and survive. Parents can handle it when you say something really dumb. "After all, he's only a kid," they'll say. If you do something stupid, they are a lot less forgiving.

"I can't believe that girl ate that whole bowl of artificial fruit."
"I know, dear, but it sure was fun watching her try to peel that banana."
"Yes, but I don't think we ought to let our little Lee go out with her. Who knows where she might take him to eat!"

Talking with the parents has dragged on and on. You've been polite, complimentary, and agreeable. You've done it all with sincerity and kept sarcasm out of your voice. Just when you think that you'll never get out of there, your date comes in and is ready to go. Finally, you are on your way.

That's how life seems sometimes. Like you're killing time, waiting around trying not to do or say something stupid. Well, you will. Do or say something stupid, that is. And wait.

Waiting is hard work. And as we said earlier, one of a teenager's main purposes in life is to avoid hard work. So if waiting is hard, quit waiting.

You see, the key is to not be waiting for life but to be living it. Experiencing it moment by moment. You need to learn to enjoy the present, not endure it as a prelude to the big event.

There are many things we look forward to in life—graduation, going off to college or work, getting married, and so on. And it's fun to think about them. But don't live the rest of your life as if it were a waiting room. It is not. The Bible tells us, "This is the day the Lord has made, let us rejoice and be glad in it." So do that. Learn to enjoy just being by yourself. Learn to enjoy being alone with God. Though God is like a parent to us in the way that He cares, God is also like a friend with whom we can be totally honest. We can always be ourselves in God's living room.

We don't have to be polite, complimentary, or agreeable. As a matter of fact, we can be impolite, uncomplimentary, and disagreeable. And God still understands. That makes the waiting not so bad.

Try, then, to really live, not just wait. Take this day and live it to its fullest. You'll find that waiting time becomes less and living time becomes more. And there are no awkward gaps in the conversation, either.

Lesson 6: Conversation

"Talk is cheap because supply exceeds demand."

—Anonymous

"Except on the first date."

—Anonymous Teenager

You open the door. Your date steps through it. You close it carefully and stand on the porch, letting the cool evening breeze wash over your face. You have survived the planning, asking, checking, being checked, and waiting. Finally, you are going on the date. The moment you've been dreading, er, I mean, desiring, is here. You are alone with your beloved—or at least someone you really like.

This first part of the date really is a lot like the opening quarter of a football game. That's when each team tries to find out as much as possible about the other. Of course, *they* do it by running different kinds of offensive and defensive plays—play action passes, reverses, stunts, and blitzes. You do it in a more subtle way. You use conversation.

While talking with your date, you try to find out as much as you can about her or him and at the same time not give away too much about yourself. You don't want to do that until you know your date better. And once you do, you may not want her or him to know anything about you. Especially your address and phone number.

The first part of the date is often the hardest and most awkward because of the following:

You don't know what to say.

You thought it was hard talking to your date's *parents?* It will be even harder to talk with your date. You only had to be with the parents for a little while. Now you're going to be with someone for hours. You want to be liked. You are worried you will say something stupid. You probably will. You are not quite sure how to start the conversation. You don't want to say anything too silly in case your date is the serious type and at the same time you don't want to say anything overly serious in case your date tends toward the silly. This puts you at a disadvantage. Since dating can be like football, think about what the team would do to get ready for a big game. Think of everything. Then do what they do. Use all available resources.

The first thing a football team does before a game is get a scouting report. Coach LaPorte sends Assistant Coaches Jones and Brown to opponents' games to see how they play, find out what their strengths and weaknesses are, and discover whether or not their uniforms are nicer. While you may not have an assistant date coach, you know people who have scouted your date before, albeit probably unintentionally. Use them. They have all kinds of knowledge you need if you are going to be successful. These folks could be friends of yours who once dated the person you're going out with, other couples who double-dated with them, or just their friends. Use them to find out likes, dislikes, hobbies, and so on.

The second thing a team uses to its advantage is diagrammed plays like the one on page 128.

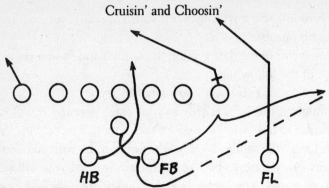

Cruisin' and Choosin'

HB   FB   FL

This is a play action pass

Well, to help you out, I've diagrammed the opening play of your date two ways for you—one good, one bad. Of course, they don't look quite like football plays, but then dating is a little different than football, though both can be contact sports. We'll look at the bad one first.

Bad Opening Play on a Date

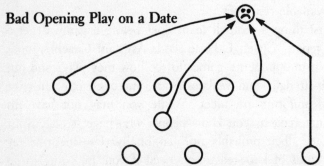

The first play opens with the following line "Well, we are finally alone. Your parents are such dips. You wouldn't believe the dumb questions they asked me while I was waiting for you."

Notice from the diagram that this is a short play. Nobody likes to have their parents criticized on the first date. The datee may complain about his or her folks, but you shouldn't. This is a right reserved for later in the relationship. A lot later. Like when you don't mind if *they* criticize *your* family.

Good Opening Play on a Date

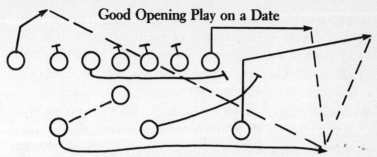

The second play goes something like this. "It sure is nice to finally be alone with you. While I enjoyed getting to know your folks and all the scintillating conversation we had, I could hardly wait until you were ready."

This opening allows the conversation to continue along a number of different lines. For example, if your date says, "Are you for real? Those people are nerds and I couldn't believe the stupid things they were asking you, like I am so mortified," you can reply, "Yeah, like totally," and the conversation is off and running.

Likewise, if your date says, "I am so glad you enjoyed yourself. Mother and Father have been looking forward so to meeting you and wrote their questions down weeks in advance," you know to hurry and get the date over with so that you can get this 40-year-old teenager home as quickly as possible. You want to go out with someone who acts his or her age, not your parents' age.

Seriously, though, conversation—good conversation, that is—is at the crux of a good relationship. Pregnant pauses are okay in soap operas, but they're death on a date. And dates can be hard enough without "not talking" them to death.

Talking with people is how you get to know all about them. You're getting the information from them, not a second or third party. They tell you what bores or excites them. They are the ones telling you what they like to do or hate doing. You can learn surprising things about people by talking to them. You might find that someone you thought was kind of stuffy is just the opposite. You may discover someone other people think is dull, is really a lot of fun—and a person you'd like to spend a lot of time with.

Talking with God requires conversation, too. Not just talking to Him about you and what's on your mind, but listening, too. God is a lot bigger than we can imagine. His thoughts are often way beyond our ability to comprehend at a quick glance. So, if you want to get to know God, take time to converse. Let the communication go both ways. You may discover a part of God you never knew existed. Be sure you listen to what He says to you about His likes and dislikes, His dreams and visions.

You'll find conversation with God, as with other people, gets easier the more you do it. The awkwardness will pass. You won't need a scouting report or diagrammed plays. God accepts your relationship wherever you choose to begin. The important thing is choosing to begin. Ready to talk?

•• 22 ••

Lesson 7: Try, Try Again

"It takes two people to make a really good date."

The second part of the date can be a lot more fun than the first. It better be, because if it isn't, the date is doomed. I say *can be* because if the first part wasn't so good then there's a good chance there won't be a second part. Your date will get up to go to the bathroom and never come back. Either that or the silence will hang so heavy that it can be cut with a plastic knife and each of you will be praying for the evening to end.

If you have had a hard time on the first part of the date, you probably feel like giving up. Don't. Keep at it. Try, try again. After all, nothing succeeds like excess. Keep on keeping on. What's the worst that can happen? If your date is already a disaster, what's to lose? Try harder. Maybe you can make the date an even bigger disaster.

Seriously, even if you are failing, at least you're doing *something*. You're more than a spectator watching it on TV. You're out there in the middle of life, living it. You're not propped back in the La-Z-Boy scoping it out on the Sony. If you were, you'd have the benefit of instant replay to see what went right or wrong. You could correct it mentally and verbally abuse the dummy on the set who made the mistake. On a date you have no such help. In real life there are no instant replays. Even though you often wish there were. At least you are out there, and not just watching it happen to others. So keep trying.

It is said that there are three kinds of people—those who watch what happens, those who make things happen, and those who wonder what happened. You are going to be one of these three. Be any one but the first. One thing I have noticed about people who just watch is that they are often critical of those who are doing. They are the ones sitting on the sidelines saying, "I can't believe he missed the throw to first," or, "That was so easy anybody could do it."

The point is, anybody isn't doing it. Somebody is. But not the know-it-all spectator. These folks usually aren't very popular. One thing about people who think they know it all is that they are annoying to those of us who do. Of course, there are lots of psychological reasons these people are the way they are, but let's face it—mostly it's because they are just a pain in the neck. Who wants to be around them? I'd rather muff the throw to first (and often have) and be playing than be sitting on my rear end criticizing those who are out there trying. Trying is a lot more rewarding than crying.

When you are one of the three, there will be a lot of times when you wonder what happened. There are times when events go speeding by as if they were Superman, you know—"faster than a speeding bullet." We're just minding our own business, watching TV or drinking a Pepsi, generally living life, and whammie—the sky falls in. Our best friend calls to remind us that the thirty-five-page term paper we didn't even know about is due first period tomorrow. The perfect date we set up for Saturday night gets chicken pox from a younger brother. We flunk algebra. "What happened?!"

Wondering what happened is scary. Sometimes we just don't have the foggiest notion what happened or why. We like to feel we are on top of things, are really aware of what's going on, and then, instead of going well everything blows up. We may try to act cool and say, "Hey, I knew that was going to happen," but mentally we are scratching our heads and saying, "Hey, no I didn't." And we usually hope it doesn't happen again. Or if it does, that we get some warning the next time.

Then there are times when we take the initiative and make things happen. That's the best kind of person to be. Even when things go wrong, we at least know what's happening. We helped make it happen. We take risks. And that's when the potential for real fun happens. How do you know you don't like [fill in the blank] until you've tried? It could be something mundane (like eating mushrooms) or really bizarre (like hunting mushrooms). How do you know you don't like to snow ski if you never have? Why are you so sure that you can't fly a plane unless you've tried?

I know you may think the last one is really far out but I live with a kid who first flew when he was 13. He wasn't sure he'd like flying (I know I don't), but he mentioned to the pilot we were with that he'd like to learn to fly someday. "What better day than today?" the pilot asked. So he showed Ben how to check magnetos, set the flaps, run up RPMs, and call the tower for clearance to take off. The next thing I knew, the pilot was sitting there with his arms folded across his chest, and my baby boy, who had never driven anything faster than a lawn tractor, had pushed the throttle to full and was steering us down the runway at eighty miles per hour.

Then he pulled back on the yoke and the next thing I knew (when I opened my eyes and quit screaming), Ben Benutti had gotten us up to a thousand feet and we were still climbing. Safely. He and I were really proud of him for trying something that scared both of us. He made something happen, and it was exciting. For all of us. Especially when we hit turbulence with our 13-year-old pilot, with ten minutes of flying time. But he brought us through that because he is (and I hope will always be) a person who makes things happen. These things may not always be fun, but they can be exciting.

The second part of a date can be exciting. If you'll take a chance. You've gotten to know the person. Now's not the time to hold back. Reveal some of yourself and you'll find that you're getting to know your date in new and exciting ways. And your date's getting to know you. Then you can start being yourself, breathing easier. And the date will be both exciting and fun.

Life, too, can be like the second part of the date. Since you are a teenager, you've already covered some of the hardest parts. Now is not the time to start playing it safe. God wants your life to be worth living and exciting. Don't be boring. Take some chances for your faith and life.

I doubt that any of the disciples ever said their lives were boring after they encountered Jesus. At times they may have wished life were a little boring and that they were back on their boats or up in sycamore trees. But I really don't think so. Because even though their lives were not always fun, they were exciting. They traveled the world. They came into contact with both royalty and common folk. They were known as the men who turned the world upside down. They made things happen.

Rest assured that God is with you in the comfortable and the uncomfortable. He is with you whether you are watching things happen or wondering what happened. But He is with you most when you are working with Him, making things happen. So—what's happening?

•• 23 ••

Lesson 8: A Break in the Action

"Okay men, I know the first half was a little rough, but I think we've still got a chance. They're not fighting back as much as they were. We're wearing them down. Stay on the attack and make each minute count. Now let's go over the assignments. Mike, you've got the popcorn and Laura. Mark, take the soda to Lisa. Jeff, you cover Kristy and the Jujyfruits. Ready, set, break!"

At a football game, halftime is signaled by the firing of a gun and the band taking the field. On a date it is a little more subtle than that—usually, that is. I have heard of guys who pulled guns, and I dated a girl who ran off with the band, but that doesn't happen often. There are ways to know when your date is about half over, though. Some of them are simple, some more complex. We'll begin with the simple ones first, since most of us fit into that category a good bit of the time.

Simple Halftime Signals

1. You've been invited to (a) go out to eat and (b) see a movie and you've just finished eating.
2. You have invited someone to (a) go to a movie and then (b) get something to eat and the movie just ended.

I realize that these were probably obvious and not very many of you needed help. The above examples were for those folks still in remedial dating. That is nothing to be ashamed of. Learning the fine points of dating is hard work. Not everyone gets it right the first time. Some of us don't get it right the four thousandth time. Those of you who have dating down so well that you are about to go pro can skip over them. The rest of us might need to write them on the blackboard a hundred times each.

That's the thing about dating. Some of it is so basic and yet we don't get it right. Maybe it's too simple. And so we need these pointers. A kind of refresher course.

A look at the more complex ways to tell if a date is half over are coming later. But first some further observations. While the complex signals are generally harder to discern (thereby earning the title "complex"), there are some things that happen which are not signals for halftime. Rather, they are signs that the final gun has sounded and you were too dense to know it. This is also known as lack of sensitivity. Or, if your date is not very tactful, just plain stupid. These are:

1. Your date falls asleep.
2. Your date starts snoring.
3. Your date starts snoring and is not asleep.
4. Your date leaves the movie to go get popcorn and doesn't return.

This list could go on and on. For some of us, it has. If you have been on more than three dates, you could probably add some of your own. Either because they have happened to you or you have done them to someone else. At any rate, all of the above are not "halftime" signals. They mean the game is over and the stands are empty. It is time to head for the locker room and analyze the game films to see what went wrong. If you can't discover anything that did, you have two choices: The first one is to sign up for remedial dating. The second is to sign your date up.

Now that we have covered the "simple" signals and "it's over" signals, it is time to move on to the complex signals.

Complex Signals

1. Your date excuses herself to go to bathroom and leaves her coat.
2. Your date goes to get popcorn and asks you what you want to drink.

As I said before, these signs are subtle and the above information is not guaranteed. You have to be aware of what is going on around you. Examine your surroundings and all possible clues. Is it an old or new coat? You know she'd never leave a new coat and skip out. No matter how bad a date is, not many young women are going to forfeit new clothing for the sake of leaving. If it is an old coat, though, you may be in trouble. It might just be old enough that it is worth leaving behind to get away from you.

Asking you what you want to drink is also a good signal. It generally indicates that he's coming back. I said generally, because it may be a ploy to lull you into thinking he is coming back when his intention is to call Yellow Cab, beat it home, and hide under the bed. He thinks that you think that he thinks if he asks you what you want to drink you'll think he's surely thinking of coming back. He probably is. But if he seems to be paying more attention to where the emergency exits are located than to your drink order, beware.

There are other signs that halftime is near. I don't feel that I should give them to you. I had to learn the hard way, and so I think you should, too. After all, why should you have it so much easier than me? Besides, I was never too good at picking up subtle signals. Girls on a bad date with me usually had to write "Take

me home. Now!!" on the business end of a shovel and hit me with it before I was aware of what was happening.

Rest assured, though, that every date has a halftime. The hard part is deciding when it is. One final clue—it will usually be some time when you are left alone. If you find that you are being left alone a lot on the date, either your date has a weak bladder or you're not much fun. I can't help you with either of those.

Halftime on a date can be as helpful and useful as halftime at the big game. At the game the half is the time when the coach gets the football team into the locker room for some rest and discussion of strategy. There's a break in the action. It is time to reflect. To change plans. To go to the bathroom. So, too, is the halftime of a date. It is when you take time to take a breather from being witty and charming. You're alone and can be yourself. You can relax and breathe again. You can also look over your game plan and see if it is getting you where you want to go. Are you having a good time? Is your date having a good time, too? If so, no changes need to be made. If not, it may be a time for drastic overhaul of the plan. If your heart is singing Dandy Don Meredith's "Monday Night Football" version of "Turn out the lights, the party's over . . ." you can make it over. That's the nice thing about a date—you can end it at the half if you both want. There's no Un-datesman-like penalty for not finishing the thing. If the "Fightin' Warthogs" are down 850 to 0 they have no such advantage. They have to play the game till the clock has ticked its last tock. And for the team, those last thirty minutes seem like decades. You, on the other hand, can take your date home.

In life, like dating and football, we all need to take breathers. We all need halftimes. Time to just rest. Time to look back on what we've done and what we want to do next. We've got a good example. At the end of each day of creation, God took some time and looked back at what He had done. *Sea monsters, every living creature that moves, and winged birds. Not a bad day's work.* I'll bet that's what He thought at the end of day five. He was checking out what He had done to see if it was what He wanted. It was. The way we humans have messed up what He created, I can only say that I'm glad He looked then and not now.

In life, halftime can be anytime. Especially since we never really know when halftime is for us. We need time out to take stock of where we've been, what we've done, and where we are going. God can help us. As we reflect, together with God we can plan where we want to go with our lives. All through the Bible we see examples of God helping people who needed that kind of help. And since He is going to be the same today and tomorrow as He was yesterday, we can be sure that He will help us.

Take a halftime today. Review your game films and replan whatever needs it. Then take a deep breath. It's time to get back to the greatest date of all time—your date with life.

·· 24 ··

Lesson 9: What's the Option?

"Tonight was so very special. Years from now I'll look back on this evening—and throw up."

You're sitting there wondering, *Have I read the signs right? Were those simple signals really simple? Is it halftime or is the date over? I think it was a complex signal. I hope it was. Am I still on a date or not?* Finally you can breathe again. Your date comes out of the bathroom and sits at the table or is shuffling down the darkened aisle laden with popcorn and pop. Whew! The third quarter has started.

I hope that during halftime you've made any adjustments necessary to ensure the date is a successful one. Now you'll find out whether or not your plans will work. Did you fine-tune things enough? You'll know shortly.

For example: It was obvious to you that your date was not enjoying the movie. People in the theater noticed it as well and had the usher come up to you and complain about your date's snoring. At halftime you looked at several options.

1. You could let her sleep. She obviously needs the rest and will feel kindly toward you later because you were so considerate.

I mean, you know that it couldn't be being with you that put her to sleep. Not with *your* personality. So let her snooze.

2. You might stuff a rag in her mouth. Gag her. This would keep the noise from disturbing the rest of the audience and the projectionist in the soundproof booth. Upon waking, however, your date may not find this very amusing. Of course, you'll never know, since she won't be able to tell you.

3. You could wake her up and suggest that since you are bored too maybe you should both leave and go someplace else more exciting—like to the local diner for a cup of coffee.

4. You could just forget about it, relax, and enjoy the movie. There's no sense in everybody having a bad time.

Let's say you picked option number three. Personally, I think that this is the best one—if you drop the sarcastic last comment. Let's look at why the others are not so good. The first one is not because when she wakes up she will be embarrassed about falling asleep on you in the first place. There are subtle ways to wake someone and act like you didn't know they were asleep anyhow. A nudge will do. Besides, if they're asleep and you get engrossed in the movie, when it is over you might forget you were with someone. As the credits roll, you get up, stroll down the aisle, head out the exit, fire up the Ford, and head home. At 2:00 A.M., you sit bolt upright from a sound sleep and say, "I think I forgot something at the theater. Let's see, was it my jacket? My wallet? My date?"

Lots of people wake up with their tongue and teeth feeling kind of fuzzy. That's fairly normal and acceptable. Unless that is because the fuzz is real and comes from being gagged with your date's handkerchief. That's cause for justifiable homicide in thirty-seven states and most foreign countries. So, with your quick wit, you probably have deduced the reason option number two is not a good idea. In case you haven't, here it is: You like living. Do this to your date and you won't be. Living, that is.

"They'll kill you dead," as my little Tim says. And no jury will convict them.

Number four is not good because you didn't go on a date to have a good time by yourself. If you had, you could have saved the price of your date's admission. Also, your date won't forgive you if you have a good time and he or she doesn't. Don't ask why, that's just the way it is. It has something to do with the old saying that "Missouri loves company," though I don't know what geography and the states have to do with dating.

So you have wisely picked option number three. You've gotten your date awake, suggested you go do something more fun, and made it to the car. Now is when you find out whether you chose correctly or not. If, as soon as she sits down in the car, she falls asleep again, chances are it was not a good plan. She could have slept in the theater in a reclining seat and you would at least have had the chance to see which teenager, who had been dodge-balled to death in the darkened gymnasium on a Halloween Friday night (which was the 31st, which backwards is the 13th, which everybody knows stands for Friday the 13th) thirty years ago by his deranged Phys Ed teacher, keeps coming back to off the teenagers of Millard Filmore High today. At this time, dig your ticket stub out of the lint at the bottom of your pocket, lock your date safely in the car, and watch the rest of the mass murders.

If, however, your date awakens like someone coming back from the dead and is genuinely interested in being with you, then you have made the right choice. Your plan is working. Instead of being doomed to disaster, you are on your way to a good time.

Sometimes in life, we wonder if the adjustments we've made were the right ones. Did we choose the correct option? Will what we decided or dreamed about turn out the way we want? We don't find out until we start living them. It's times like these that we need to ask God's help. He'll be with us as we look at our plans for life. We may think we have everything mapped out in advance. Some of us like it that way. Later we find out that we need to make some adjustments along our way. Planning is good, as long as we don't get so committed to following the plan that we miss out on the interruptions that are bound to happen.

Life is never quite as neat and organized as we wish it was. Interruptions do happen. Sometimes the interruptions to our plans make life really exciting. Delightful surprises we would never have taken time out for. New friends to meet and new experiences. Neatness does not always count in life. And life is really more of an art than a science. You can't plan it out to the last little detail and expect it to follow that path. It just won't happen.

Likewise, God is not going to send you, for every prayer prayed and 3,500 proofs of purchase of the King James Bible, a detailed plan of exactly how your life will go. Sometimes we all wish He would. In reality, I doubt that we would like it. After all, at times it's the surprises in life that are the most fun. The unexpected keeps things exciting.

Nope, God won't send you a road map to your life, detailing what is going to happen to you on May 11, 1998, and whether you are going to make the best choice about what to do that day. What God does promise is to be with you and help you make the necessary adjustments—even when they mean 180-degree turnarounds in your life's plans.

The unexpected does occur. It is one of two constants in our lives. Sometimes it happens when we are teenagers, like when the college we've planned on going to won't accept us or we don't like the major we've planned on all of our lives. Sometimes the unexpected happens to us when we are older and set in our ways.

The other constant is that God is there—even when we mess up the plans. Even when we pick the wrong option. That's because He loves us—even when we don't plan too well, or fail to think about where our plans might take us. Psalm 107 has a verse that really applies to our lives. After talking about people who obeyed and disobeyed God and telling how God rescued them all when they called on Him, the last verse says that we should remember the record of God's enduring love. I know that's my favorite record. I think it's probably God's greatest hit. If we love God and are trying to follow Him, no matter how our plans turn out, He is there.

25

Lesson 10: Turn Out Your Lights— Your Date Life Is Over

sleep /'slep/ *n* : a state or period of reduced activity accompanied by a complete or partial unconsciousness
bad date /bahd dat/ *n* see SLEEP

Actually, it's not that bad. Your dating life isn't over—yet. The path to dating success so far has been laced with many pitfalls. If you have made it this far, you've done well. You have not fallen into any of them and you will be seen again. Seen again, that is, if you manage to get over the final obstacle to dating happiness. Ending the date. This is the hard part. Everything up to this point has been a mere speed bump on the freeway of love compared to ending the date. But all good (and thank heavens, bad) things must come to an end. One is rapidly approaching. Either the date will end well or you will end with it. The date is over. Time is running down. The question is "How do I end it—and walk away unscathed?"

Now that I've gotten you good and scared, don't panic. Of course, that's easy for me to say, I'm not on a date (haven't been able to get one in years). If it's a good date, ending is easier. Much easier. In some ways, that is. In others, if it has been good, really good, you don't want it to end and so it's hard. If you are wondering whether you've had a good time on the date, a good rule of thumb is if you are thinking, *I wish it would never end*, then you've been on the date of your life. If your thoughts run more along the lines of, *I wish we had a little more time*, well, then it's been a good date. Not great, but probably three stars. If every bone in your body is screaming, *I wish it had ended before it began*, chances are you did not have a good time.

One way to end a date is to kiss good-night. Unless you are a real good kisser; then the date seems to have a very hard time winding down. If you are a bad kisser, the date will end itself.

"To kiss, or not to kiss." That's the big question. At least it is at the end of a date. Well, to some of us it is a big question. For some others, the date itself has been nothing but one long kiss, interrupted by movies, munchies, and Mother. If your date has been one of these kissing marathons, then your big question is "How do I know which one was the good-night kiss? Or should we just shake hands to officially end it?" That would be something different.

The hard thing about kissing your date good-night (once you've answered the big question in the affirmative) is the timing. When do you do it? Do you kiss good-night in the car, alone? If you do, walking your date to the door and shaking his or her hand seems like a real letdown. Which makes you feel as if the date wasn't quite as good as you thought it was up to that point. If, however, you wait until you get to the door, just when you are ready to lock lips the porch light will come on and Julie, your date's youngest sister, will wander out and ask, "Whatcha doin'?" This is not an accident. You should have picked up on this the fifteenth time it happened. What is going on is this—your date's parents have kept this kid up seven hours past her bedtime just for this moment. Even though they used to kiss (obviously, since kissing is one of the preliminaries before the final round that produces babies. I realize this was awfully scientific, but trust me, it's true), they don't want you doing it to their little girl or boy. And of course it is, from their point of view, always you doing it to their child, even if he or she has you pinned against the garage door with your eyes and lips wide open.

Also, when kissing, aim is important. If you both tilt your heads the same way, you can't kiss. You might hit a nose if you're lucky. If you are having trouble tilting your heads in opposite directions to make interlip location possible, that could also be a clue that maybe you're just not ready for this step yet. Lovers usually do have some sense of what to do next and it turns out right. If you don't believe me, go to the movies. Cinematic lovebirds never kiss each other's noses by accident. If you keep missing each other's lips, then give it up and just *say* good-night. Don't even try for a handshake. You might end up grabbing an ear.

If the date has not gone so well, ending it requires more delicacy. A lot more. You don't want to hurt your date's feelings. Even if you really do, there is something to be said for being nice. Right now, I can't recall what it is, but I'm sure there is. At least that's what my mom told me.

Oh, yeah, I know what it is. (Just kidding, Mom.) You want to be nice and thoughtful, because if you are mean and nasty, your date will tell every other guy or girl at school, including the one you really want to like you, and nobody will go out with you. And your date's grandmother will tell her best friend who will tell your grandmother and then even *she* won't like you, and if your grandmother's not on your side, "Let me tell you, kid" (as my grandmother always says), nobody will be. I mean, how can anyone like someone whose own grandmother doesn't like him?

So now that you know you should always be nice, because if you aren't, Grandma Bill will get you, read on for things to avoid.

Ways Not to End a Bad Date

Do not say, "I haven't had this much fun since I had pneumonia."

Do not say, "When we go by your house, I'll slow down and you jump out."

Do not just slow down and throw your date out.

Do not burn rubber and scream, "Free at last," as you leave.

Do not say, "That was fun, let's do it again some decade."

Do not say, "Your sister looks real cute. Is she doing anything next Friday?"

Be nice. The following are things you can do.

Ways to End a Bad Date

Do say, "Thank you for going out with me." She didn't have to you know. And probably would have had a better time if she hadn't.

Walk her to the door.

Be polite.

I know it's a short list. But being nice doesn't have to be that hard. Just think of all the times you were having a miserable time and wished someone would be nice to you. Here's a chance to do unto another what you wish others had done unto you.

Soon you will be on your way home. The date will have ended. You will be able to look back and reflect. Some parts will make you smile, from the inside out. I hope most of it will. Some things, as you remember them, may make you cringe. Whatever the case, now you will do a kind of mental "Date in Review," with anchorperson (put your name here).

Doing such a review, taking stock of the situation, is good. Good, that is, as long as we learn to accept our successes and our failures and learn from them both. If all we do is dwell on the situation, then we do no one any good—especially ourselves. We can ruminate ourselves into ruin by replaying all of our mistakes. Look at them and accept them and move on. On the other hand, we need to savor our successes. That's the fun part. Enjoy what you enjoyed and did well.

We need to use all of the experiences God allows to come our way to learn something—about ourselves, others, and God. Each experience in life can teach us a lot, if we will let it. We can see what mistakes we made so that we can avoid them in the future. We can go over what we did right, what turned out the way we wanted it to, and see what we need to do to have that happen in the future.

God can help us in that. If we ask for the help, that is. Too often we think and think and think and never ask God what it all means. How can we take what we've experienced and learn from it? That's the mark of successful people. They learn to avoid past pitfalls and keep moving toward happy, fulfilled lives.

Yes, God wants to help us. Ask for His illumination daily. That way you will be able to live life to its fullest. Right up to the end.

26

Lesson 11: Breakin' Up Is Hard to Do

"They say that breaking up is hard to do.
It's just as hard now as it was in '62."

—with apologies to Neil Sedaka

Breaking up *is* hard to do. And, sad to say, breaking up is as much a part of dating as asking someone out in the first place. Not every relationship could be turned into the love story of the decade. Not every one should be.

We met the summer of our junior year. Her name was Jeanie. She was traveling with a choir and I fell in love with her the first time I saw her. She was pretty, witty, and charming. She looked good in a football jersey or a silk dress. We liked the same music, books, and Peanuts comic strips. She was Lucy ("I love mankind. It's people I can't stand") and I was Snoopy ("Joe Cool, the author"). We wrote every day—letters, postcards, anything we could get our hands on. When we could con our parents into paying for it, we called each other on the phone. She even came to visit me at homecoming. We were in love. There was just one minor problem: We lived 140 miles apart. She in Indiana and I in Ohio. A Hoosier and a Buckeye. A modern Romeo and Juliet. In love, but separated by three solid hours of freeway transit.

We endured for a while. Almost a year, as a matter of fact. Finally, the letters became less loving and more friendly. We began dating other people. I went to her graduation. She sent me a gift. A record. I still have it. When fall rolled around we both went to college. She to Indiana University in south-central Indiana and I to a small school in northern Ohio. Should have been the end, but it wasn't.

We began writing again. Two friends away at college and rather lonely. In our letters we began to reminisce about the times we had spent together. We started calling each other. Still long-distance, but no parental permission needed. We got more and more serious. More and more loving. More and more passionate. Our spring breaks happened to overlap so she invited me to I.U. for the few days before they let out. I went. Those days were happy, joyous ones. We went for walks in the daytime and evening. We sat and talked for hours. It was delightful. I was back in her world and was reminded over and over again why I had been attracted to her in the first place. She was fun. She was smart. She was pretty. She was easy to be with. The love we had experienced before was back in full bloom. I was so happy. So was she. So I thought.

When I got back to college there was a letter waiting for me. It was from Jeanie. In it she said she had enjoyed seeing me again, but . . . but she wanted to just be friends. She realized that now. She had thought she was in love with me, but she was wrong. She had only been in love with the idea of being in love. Could we still be friends?

I thought I would die. I called her immediately. I told her I would die. I begged and pleaded. It did no good. She hung up. After that, she wouldn't take any of my phone calls and didn't answer any of my letters. She did send just one more letter. I found it just the other day, dog-eared and tear-stained, its bright pink stationery all faded and old-looking. In it was a poem that said, in its last line, "Please don't die." Well, even though I felt like it, I didn't.

You meet someone. She's witty, pretty, and charming. You ask her out. Again and again and again. You fall in love. Your life revolves around her. Then you break up. It happens to all of us. And it hurts. No matter how old you get, how many times it has happened, it hurts. Bad.

It's a tragic scenario, but all too real. For some of us it is more real than for others. Some folks seem to fall in love and it lasts forever. From their first date they are inseparable. They hit it off perfectly and their life together goes smoothly. Or at least appears to. We envy them. For the rest of us, it usually doesn't happen that way. Love's road is often rocky. Something doesn't quite click, we don't match up as much as we thought we would. Usually one party recognizes it before the other, and so, wants to break it off.

It feels as though the world is ending. And, in some ways it is. Our world with that person, at least. If you've felt really in love, you have imagined lots of things about the other person. So this fantasy world, this daydreaming you've done about the future, is no longer profitable. As a matter of fact, the dreams may come back to haunt you. You think of all the things you've said. How you've let that person into your life. She's become a part of you. And now she is destroying what you gave her. She doesn't want to have anything to do with the plans and dreams and hopes you have.

You've enjoyed her company and looked forward to talking with or just being with her. Now it's over. You're alone. And lonely. You don't feel like talking to anyone. You feel that there isn't anyone who can know how you are feeling. You're right. Others have felt that pain, but yours is unique to you. No one else can feel what you are feeling.

That's the reality. Sometimes it hurts so bad you just want to die. Maybe you even feel that you *will* die. That's the bad news.

The good news is that you won't. Even if you wish you could. You will live to love another day. It doesn't seem like it. And you may not even want to. But you will. Someone else will come along. And no, you will never forget the other person you loved. But the pain will ease as the joy of the new relationship takes its place. You may find yourself wondering what happened to the other person and be sad that it ended. Or you may find yourself wondering why you thought that relationship was so great when you compare it to what you have now.

When you break up, learn to rely on your friends. After all, you're not the first person this ever happened to, even if it feels that way. And while no one may be able to really understand the particular grief you're experiencing, everyone has lost at love. At least once. Sometimes more. They can empathize and be with you. They'll realize that you need to be sad sometimes. But they also know that you need to laugh and fool around and start living again. Especially when you don't want to.

Also, learn to be yourself. Far too often, when we are "in love" we project a false image of ourselves to the other person. We are afraid that if that person really knew us she wouldn't like us. Some people won't. But others will. Practice being yourself. Let your uniqueness shine through. It is, after all, what makes you you and special. And you are special.

There's one more thing you need to do. After learning to be yourself, learn to like the person you are. You are complete as you are. You are whole, whether you are with someone or alone, in love or in between love. Another person may help you feel more complete, and when a special relationship develops, you will be. But you can stand alone, if you learn to like yourself. And if you like yourself, you'll find that you are more attractive to others. Your self-confidence and assurance will come through.

Love is a funny thing. Funny ha-ha and funny weird.

Sometimes it's funny both ways at the same time. It seems that the harder we try to find it and impress somebody, the less likely we are to win that person's love. And when we're not trying at all, it happens to us. I think there's a lesson there for us. See if you can figure it out.

If you want love to last, you must like the person you love. Sounds silly, I know. But don't give up on me yet. Think about it. If you like someone it is easier to love him, because you already know him, and the way he eats or dresses or anything else isn't a surprise and won't bother you as much as it might later. Sometimes, when we fall in love, the things that first attracted us to someone drive us crazy later. Her laugh, his haircut, her clothes, his scent, her smartness, his silliness. Some of that stuff gets plain annoying. If we just love, and don't like, that is.

When we break up, sometimes it is because the other person sees that the image we've been projecting isn't quite true. Let's face it, when you're in love, you try too hard sometimes. People like genuine folks. People who are themselves. And who don't try to live up to some lover's expectations. Or imagination.

So use the pain of breaking up, as hard as it is, to learn to like yourself. Learn to be yourself. Stop the negative, "If I were only like. . . ." You aren't. And that's okay. In fact, it is better than okay. It's great. You want to fall in love with someone who likes you for you. And you need to like the other person as is. Love is not some sort of project where you shape your boyfriend or girlfriend into the ideal. For one thing, there is no ideal. Second, if you don't like him the way he is, why are you going with him? You want to be able to be yourself, say what you want to say, relax, and enjoy life. When that kind of relationship happens, love is worth waiting for. Even on the long nights when it doesn't seem so.

Breaking up is hard to do, but it just could be God's way of helping us avoid the trap of phoniness and being stuck in a relationship that limits our potential. Sure it hurts. Growth and change usually do. I wish they didn't. But I have learned that I'd rather hurt and change than hurt and hurt and hurt and feel trapped in a relationship that hurts everyone involved.

So, even though breaking up is hard, grow through it. And hold out for real love. A love that lets you be you. Because with that kind of love, you'll make it through all of life's storms. It is what makes life, and love, worth living.

·· *27* ··

"Goodnite, Sweetheart, Goodnite"
—The Spaniels, 1954

"Now I lay me down to sleep
I pray the Lord my soul to keep.
If I should die before I wake
At least I won't make any more mistakes."

—Brent Bill, 1954 to present

The day is finally over. You've done enough hangin', foolin', cruisin', and choosin' for twenty teenagers. It's all you can handle in one twenty-four-hour period. Maybe it's time to crawl into bed. You know, to get some rest—so you can start all over again tomorrow.

It is one thing we all need. Rest, that is. As much as we like to think we are SuperTeen ("Faster than a speeding ticket, more powerful than a little brother, able to eat a Big Mac in a single bite—strange visitor from another planet—It's SuperTeen. Fighting for truth, justice, and the right to stay out past midnight on weekends"), our bodies are not invincible. Though we may think we can shop or bop till we drop, we will usually drop before we think we will. We need to take a break, catch our breath, let our bodies replenish themselves, all so we can go run ourselves ragged tomorrow. Needing to rest is nothing to be ashamed of.

After all, being a teenager is hard work. Some of it is mental. No, I don't mean like doing homework or taking the SAT. I mean like preparing to go on the big date. Remember all those lessons, earlier? All the things you had to remember to do right and steps to follow. That's enough to wear out anybody's mind. Part of the hard work of being a teen is physical. No, not like cleaning your room or shoveling the snow off the front walk. You know better than to do stupid things like that. That would give all teenagers a bad name. What I mean is the really physically difficult stuff—like balancing all those cups of Coke while walking back to your seat at the football game. And then there are the combination shots, physical and mental at the same time. Such as trying to decide which pattern of toilet paper looks best as you drape it through your boyfriend's assorted trees and shrubbery.

"Well, Konda, do we go with a crisscross pattern or drape it like Christmas tree tinsel?"

Sometimes we feel like we can go on and on and on, but we can't. There comes a time when our bodies say to our minds, "Whoa buddy, I've had enough. You can go on without me, 'cause I'm going to lay down here and take a little nap." And suddenly we find that we can sleep anywhere—on top of kitchen countertops, propped up in the backseat of the team's bus, or in the middle of a "Bonzo Dog Doo Dah Band" concert.

At other times it's our minds that just shut down. They are too worn-out with thinking to think another thought. Our bodies may have been idle, but our brains have been on overtime. They've been looking at everything imaginable from every conceivable angle and are just plain tuckered out. The body is saying, "Come on, let's cruise the mall just one more time," and the brain is saying, "If you're going, you're going alone, because . . . ZZZZzzzzzz."

Sleep is nature's way of telling us to slow down. So is death, but sleep is a much less drastic measure. It's a temporary solution to a temporary problem. If we lie down and catch a few "zzz's" we find we are ready to tackle teenage problems with renewed vim, vigor, and vitality. In other words, after a good night's sleep we feel almost ready to get out of bed.

Often when we climb into the bed (be it water or bunk), we lie still for a few minutes and think over how the day has been. We reflect on what has happened, why it happened, how it happened, and if we ever want it happening again. We also consider how we could have made it better. We suddenly dream up all the witty comebacks we wished we could have thought of when we were being slammed earlier. The algebra problems we've never understood suddenly become clear and we'd like to call Miss Marks up and tell her we finally understand it all. We know how happy she'd be for us, but we realize she'd probably be happier during fourth period tomorrow than now, at 12:34 A.M.

Gradually, though, we drift off to sleep. To never-never land. The land of enchantment, the domain of dreams. For some of us, our days are so intense that we continue to live them in our dreams at night. For others nighttime brings a respite from the world of the real and catapults us to the world of the unreal. Either way, it's a break from living.

And it's a break we need. We were not made to go on and on and on. We were, the Bible tells us, created in the image of God. And what did God do? He took a break. At the end of each day. And then He took a whole day off at the end of the week. So I guess that tells us how important rest is.

What is also important is that sleep brings the day to a close. Going to bed is an ending. This particular twenty-four-hour period, with all its unique glories and special strife, is over. It had a mixture of good things and horrible things—if your days are anything like mine. Some days seem to be especially good. When they are over and we lay ourselves down to sleep, we kind of hate to see them end. At other times they have been so bad we want to cry ourselves to sleep. And do. At still other times we want nothing more than to drift off blissfully into slumberland.

Whatever kind of day we have had, nighttime brings one common thing to days good or bad—finality. Closure. The day is done.

And as Scarlett O'Hara said in *Gone With the Wind*, "Tomorrow is another day." Not a bad sentiment from someone who lost her family, her plantation, the man she loved, and her whole way of life. Even if she was just a character in a book and movie. So, while that's easy for her to say, it's still true. Tomorrow *is* another day. It is the only thing that is constantly fresh and unspoiled in our lives. It is out there waiting to see what we will make of it.

So enjoy going to sleep. Let your day end. Glory in the good. Let the horrible pass into dreamland and the past. Your future is out there. It's waiting for you. And only you, with God's help, can make it the way you want it to be.

Good night